Contents

Preface

Within *European contextualising in analytical sociology and ethnographical representation on history and the present,* Remco Torenbosch (1982) researched the colour of the blue background of the European flag, its original production and history. The presentation shows a collection of textile samples made in the European blue colour code by the still existing weaving mills in the European Union. Although the colour code for the EU flags is mandated, because of the differing production processes in each country and at each mill, it can still vary, resulting in a wide diversity of blue tints, as seen in this collection. According to Torenbosch, these interpretations are a striking metaphor for the more recent European situation: "The idea of Europe is not a collective concept, and it certainly can not be defined. Each member country has different ideas about its meaning. ... The colour differences reflect the diversity in expectations and visions."

In a physical sense the European blue colour works like a monochrome in modernist tradition: with its purity, desire for transcendence, and an optimistic belief in utopian potential. At the same time, in psychological sense the blue functions like a blue projection screen on which diverse and critical ideas about Europe and the European Union can be projected. By also functioning as a survey of an almost vanished European textile industry – which has largely moved to rising economies such as India, and within the next two decades will have disappeared entirely from Europe – the result of this research is not only a collection of cultural objects, it is above all else, a consciousness-raising exercise regarding the European experiment, which in post-war thinking was established as a union for peace and greater economic stability.

Searching for Blue in a Union Flag
by Charles Esche

Remco Torenbosch has adopted the European Union (EU). Or, at least, he has adopted its most familiar symbol and turned it into a research-based artwork. This is no easy feat for something which purports to be instantly recognisable, so much so that it has become the unremarkable backdrop to many stage-managed political summits of the blue suited, monochrome frocked elite that pass for the EU leadership. These unimpressive gatherings have become the means through which the EU communicates to its citizens in ways that serve mostly to emphasise how most EU politicians lost their spark and personal touch in the process of attaining their positions. In this bleak picture, Torenbosch has picked up on the flag as his subject as a direct means of perceiving what might be at stake and revealing what remains unquestioned. In the process he gives the EU flag a character of its own, complete which the quirks and idiosyncracies so often lacking in the politicians and bureaucrats themselves. Through formal means, the artist seems to be suggesting that we might have been looking in the wrong place to understand the kind of European Union that has been built. Perhaps the symbols of the EU are the clue to determining what the Europe of the twenty-first century might be, for better or worse.

Torenbosch's work traces the development of the EU flag and its iterations across the Union. The story of its design, its symbolism, the arguments over, and construction of, its iconography after the suicidal European war of the 1940s all speak of a particular history and regional sense of place. The blue that approaches the old Roman imperial purple but shies away from it at the same time speaks ambivalently about Europe's place in the world today. The 12 stars, marking not the number of member states as in the US flag, but uncertainly signifying something related to Catholic Christian symbolism (while at the same time never being officially acknowledged), seem to be pregnant with the difficulties that the EU faces in understanding its continental and global role today.[1] The fact that the flag was itself designed for another organisation and simply adopted by default are all a piece with the ambiguity that seems to always overwhelm any deeper analysis of EU mythology.[2] The regional diversity of the blue itself, represented by the artist's inclusion in his work of so many versions of the flag manufactured in different states and often far beyond the EU borders, point out a paradoxical lack of standardisation within a rule-based, juridical community that imposes its will through the courtroom rather than the debating chamber. In Torenbosch's hands then, searching for the blue in the union flag becomes a political odyssey through the difficulties of being part of, and expressing, European unionism through collective means.

As an artwork, it seems to me to reach back to the problematising discourse around political symbolism that characterised Anglo-American cultural studies in the 1980s with such works as Paul Gilroy's *There Ain't No Black in the Union Jack* or the early dub poetry of Linton Kwezi Johnston. These projects, also explored in the USA by African-American artists like David Hammons, tried to undermine the symbolism of national images and reveal their imperialist or racist roots in order to replace or reinvent them. While Torenbosch's project is much less overtly political, it nevertheless opens up the possibility of a discussion about EU symbols that are often obscured by bureaucratic strategies of avoidance. By searching for a flag and a colour, the artist reveals some of the loaded assumptions behind a simple piece of cloth and allow the continuing ambivalences and discontents of the EU to be approached from another angle altogether—an angle that might offer a more fruitful route to understanding how contemporary culture can play a part in reshaping European ideas in the future.

1
The International Pan-European Union is the oldest European unification movement. It is independent of all political parties, but has a set of principles by which it appraises politicians, parties, and institutions. The International Pan-European Union has four main basic principles: liberalism, Christianity, social responsibility, and pro-Europeanism. At the same time, it openly welcomes and acknowledges the contributions of Judaism and Islam whose heritage they share.

2
The advent of an elected European Parliament in 1979 saw the launch of a new initiative to find a European Community flag - and on 28 April 1983 the European Parliament decreted that the Council's flag should be Europe's official emblem. It was adopted by the European Council in Milan on 29 June 1985 and has been used by the European Union since 1986.

The Blue Curtain
by Mihnea Mircan

Remco Torenbosch's ongoing project is an oblique look at post-1989 Europe, with the blue flag of the European Union (EU) as allegorical segue. The project inventories, the different shades of blue produced in Europe's cheaper workshops, where economic expediency and colour-code miscalibration destabilise or corrode the symbol, withdraw from the flag the uniform quality it aspired to: that of a vera icon of European communality, an impression of the reconciliatory, cloudless sky overlooking it.[1] Were they assembled diachronically, these chromatic flickers would work like stills in an abstract film, where insufficiency or excess—too much or too little blue, blue of a different kind—would register as contamination, as the various degrees to which a parasitical presence manifests itself, carrying the film into other narratives than that of sameness. The colour of the flag is never the right one: the dispute here does not seem to be so much one disuniting original and failed copies, but an endless string of imperfections from which no model can be wrested. The rhetoric of European homogeneity is pierced by machinic Freudian slips, while 'plan' and the repeated 'accidents' in its execution begin to illustrate each other's impersonal nature, to correspond to one another as the failures—gigantic or geopolitical, microscopic, technical and equally anonymous—of the same desire. Torenbosch's monochrome film and the ghostly flashes that disrupt its seamless flow document the spasms of a political construct. Within the modernist canon, the function of the monochrome is to arrest vision and confine its motion to the epiphanic concreteness of the picture plane. Invoking the diversions of Yves Klein, Blinky Palermo or Derek Jarman is of similarly limited applicability here, yet these references do bring a speculative museological dimension to Torenbosch's project. His vacant and chromatically hesitant flags might be conceived as ethnographic exhibits in a future museum of political history, artefacts that indirectly visualise social convulsions and economic disparities. There, in the 'Europe' gallery of such a museum, the flags might be installed in relation to another attempt to materialise a political figure of speech: the Iron Curtain. What the Iron Cutain had held apart, the European flag mends—the assets, transactions, debts and losses in an economy of affects and representations that unites Europe's incongruous 'halves', be they organised along East-West, or North-South axes.

It will be a matter of curatorial sensitivity to discuss, in tandem, the caesura between how subjectivities were fashioned at the two sides of the Curtain, and today's efforts to inscribe hefty bureaucracy, financial scandals, racially-motivated deportations, the continent's centres and ghettos into the same, shared political project. The Iron Curtain was of uncertain size (but presumably very large) and occupied an indeterminate location (but presumably zigzagged through the very heart of what had been, and is again, 'Europe'). The vast, intractable hiatus in political and cultural exchange it metaphorised is incommensurate with the efficiency with which this obstacle was dismantled and sent to the historiographic junkyard in 1989. The European flag too oscillates between different regimes of representation. Of imprecise size and colour, it flutters somewhere between the low-wage places where it is manufactured and the ceremonial occasions where distinct ideas of Europe, that its distinct hues of blue might be correlates for, temporarily forget what differentiates them in order to respond to some fresh crisis.

A museum is a place where a demonstration is under way, to do with how different objects register the passage of time, with the roles they are assigned in inaugurating or consolidating genealogies—the pasts from which today's citizens desire descent. In the museum, a prologue to the contemporary is both articulated and demarcated, as the anteriority from which the present inevitably proceeds. To extend this speculative thread, it might be argued that the question "what is Europe?" engenders difficul-ties not unlike those of 'the contemporary'. Rather than in itself, the contemporary is to a larger extent conceivable via an arc through the future, as the sum of alarming emergencies, moral, political, social and environmental gridlocks it accelerates towards. Europe too exists as a temporal anamorphosis, as the 'picture plane' where distinct timelines are superposed or interwoven. There is a default of the European notion, one that merges the economical or geopolitical motivations, as well as the rhetorical benefits, on which this transnational construction rests, its severe iconographic deficit and the spectral monuments that adorn Euro banknotes, its projected origin in Athenian democracy and the resolute response to today's Greece as toxic ballast. It is in times of crisis and

1
By the early twentieth century, the industry in the developed world often involved immigrants in "sweat shops", which were usually legal but were sometimes illegally operated. They employed people in crowded condi-tions, working manual sewing machines, and be-ing paid less than a living wage. This trend worsened due to attempts to protect existing industries which were being challenged by developing countries in South East Asia, the Indian subcontinent and Central America. Although globalization saw the manufacturing largely out-sourced to overseas labour markets, there has been a trend for the areas histori-cally associated with the trade to shift focus to the more white collar associ-ated industries of fashion design, fashion modeling and retail. Areas histori-cally involved heavily in the 'rag trade' include London and Milan in Europe, and the SoHo district in New York City.

anxiety that these fractured narratives and abstract obligations are made (agonic) flesh, and that another Europe embodies as a gravity-defying, hybrid body, struggling to insulate and police its suddenly perceived outer edges. Echoes of these layered stories are captured—and rendered allegorically, even if that means the allegorical simplification of an allegory that had grown beyond any coherent legibility—in the azure apathy of Torenbosch's flags.

I would like to return once more to that territory—ideological in the real world, curatorial in our makeshift museum—shared by the blue blanks of the European flag and the rusting detritus of the Iron Curtain, the info kiosks of today's statistics and the theatrical deus ex machina of the Cold War. The site where they prop each other up in museological demonstration, so that history appears as both tangible and unfolding at an imperceptible remove. If there is a precedent for this juxtaposition between ruin and displaced emblem, it might be a painting that the visitors to the Vatican often overlook: Tommaso Laureti's *Triumph of Christianity over the Pagan Idol*, spreading across the ceiling of the Hall of Constantine. This painting too inaugurated a new epoch, in ideology and image-making, it too maintained the recognisable remnants of the vanquished adversary (rather than pulverise that adversary into a fine dust), in order to reinforce the supremacy of the new effigy. Shattered to bits, Apollo's statue lies at the bottom of its former pedestal, now occupied—somewhat awkwardly—by the Crucifixion whose revelation Apollo has had. The new and the obsolete, that which begins and that which

does not end when the new occurs, appear to be dialectically inseparable in a painting that, to equal extents, represents Constantine's manoeuver to replace pagan symbols with Christian insignia and ensure the iconographic consolidation of the Empire, as well as captures the curatorial effect of Counter-Reformation politics. Rather than argued for, or expounded upon, the superiority of Christian faith is vigorously enacted, played out in the illusionistic non-site where the scene takes place and in the broken marble of the statue.

Our museum draws a temporal bridge between the current ideological vacuum, whose dutiful maintenance, one of the European Union's central concerns, and a time when Europe was producing more history than it could consume, to quote Winston Churchill's apocryphal aphorism about the Balkans. It looks at how models of European citizenship or the diffuse sense of an European self were upheld or debilitated by symbols of togetherness and declarations of war, by odes to prosperity and decrees of austerity. With the Curtain suddenly lifted in 1989, each of its sides revealed to the other incomplete identities, excessive or insufficient selves unprepared for co-optation in a story with a singular *denouement*. After the self-refutation of Eastern Communisms, understood either metonymically or prophetically as the demise of Communism, the liberal cosmology was free to unfold toward whatever messianic destiny awaited it. The disappearance of a brutally enforced paradigm of consensus and the emergence of a paradigm of indignation and reparation—with vastly different rhetorical and practical manifestations across the Eastern Bloc—was followed by the historically unique episode of another free, absolute consensus around liberalism. Throughout the 1990s, experiments in market liberalisation collided with nationalist furore, and the arias of populism were sung against the hastily executed backdrops of globalisation. The European Union papered over the fissure, and the flag designed by Arsène Heitz and Paul Lévy in 1955, with its 12 (only 12, obstinately 12) stars, was the source of desire, political vociferation and self-colonising angst. It presided over endless rehearsals of European polyphony. It was summoned, as omen or warning, in response to either the melancholy of catching up with such a future (Jurgen Habermas' "catching-up revolution" evacuates from the post-89 upheavals any radical, transformative aspirations, so they remain mere attempts to make up for lost time) or the susceptibility to embrace the providential ideologies, however patchy or corrupt, that would infuse the daily bathos with some sense of exceptionality.

Revolving around an unfixed common denominator, Remco Torenbosch's flags compress this story, as well as other European parables of disparity and appeasement, of political spaces smooth or striated. Purified and removed from their conventional festive position, the flags might be the best instrument we have to picture the alkahest of a new European sociability, and to imagine what the residue of that alchemical transformation—the making stable, porous and predictable of a continent—might be

The Eurozone crisis (often referred to as the Euro crisis) is an ongoing crisis that has been affecting the countries of the Eurozone since late 2009. It is a combined sovereign debt crisis, a banking crisis and a growth and competitiveness crisis. The crisis made it difficult or impossible for some countries in the euro area to repay or re-finance their government debt without the assistance of third parties. Moreover, banks in the Eurozone are undercapitalised and have faced liquidity problems. Additionally, economic growth is slow in the whole of the Eurozone and is unequally distributed across the member states. Governments of the states most severely affected by the crisis have coordinated their responses with a committee dubbed "the Troika" formed by three international organisations: the European Commission, the European Central Bank and the International Monetary Fund.

**Economic Fabric
by European Foundation for the
Improvement of Living and
Working Conditions (Eurofound)**

2008

The textiles industry represents a significant sector of economic activity in world trade and also within the European Union (EU). It is a highly diverse and heterogeneous industry which covers a wide variety of end products ranging from hi-tech synthetic yarns to wool fabrics, cotton bed linen to industrial filters, or nappies to high fashion. This diversity of end products corresponds to a multitude of industrial processes, enterprises and market structures. Over the past decade, in particular since the abolition of trade quotas in the sector on 1 January 2005, the European textiles sector has undergone significant changes to keep abreast of competition in the global market. The sector has also been facing increased competitive pressure due to technological changes affecting production processes, as well as end products themselves. As a result, in order to remain competitive, the industry has had to restructure and modernise itself, as well as to relocate its production to lower wage countries within and outside the EU.

Today the competitive advantage of the European textiles sector lies in its focus on quality and design, innovation and technology, and high value-added products. This, in turn, also requires adequate education and industry specific training programmes for a generally low-skilled workforce. One of the challenges that the sector is currently facing concerns the growing shortage of qualified human resources, which is most acute in the field of higher education graduates in textiles engineering. This mapping report is part of a follow-up study of initial research on the textiles sector which was carried out in 2004 and commissioned by the European Monitoring Centre on Change (EMCC). It is part of a broader sectoral study including four company case studies and two cluster studies, as well as four scenarios projecting a possible future development of the textiles sector in Europe. The aim of this mapping report is to provide a comprehensive insight into an industry in transition, highlighting also good practice examples at local, regional, national and European levels to alleviate the negative employment effects of restructuring in the sector.

While trade liberalisation, increasing competitive pressure from countries outside the EU, demographical developments, new technological developments and the introduction of new regulatory requirements certainly bring change to the European textiles sector, these changes also affect society as a whole. For instance, when a company decides to relocate manufacturing activities to Asia, or when companies boost their global competitiveness through clustering or through innovative use of new technologies, these developments have a direct effect on the job situation of workers in the region where the company is located. This, in turn, generates positive or negative welfare effects for the society. In other words, the textiles sector does not exist in isolation but is part of a socioeconomic system where it both drives change and is affected by change. In response to the requests and issues raised by the High Level Group, the Commission in October 2004 proposed seven actions to enhance the competitiveness of the European textiles industry. In December 2004, the High Level Group resumed its work to continue the debate on unfinished issues and monitor the situation of the sector in 2005. A follow-up report was adopted by the High Level Group in 2006 containing an assessment of the implementation of the 2004 recommendations, a vision for the future, as well as further recommendations.

Since 1995, quotas on international textiles trade have been progressively phased out in the EU, US and Canada. On 1 January 2005, the last quotas for textile trade under the Agreement on Textiles and Clothing (ATC) disappeared, and all WTO members, especially the developing countries, had then unrestricted access to the European, American and Canadian markets. However, in the months that followed the opening of the market, many European producers expressed concern over the sudden increase in Chinese textiles exports to the EU.

To solve this problem, the EU and China drew up an agreement in June 2005, which was set to expire at the end of 2007. The aim of the agreement was to manage the growth of Chinese textile imports to the EU by limiting the rate of imports on 10 product categories, while also allowing fair and reasonable growth for Chinese exports (European Commission, 2005). The continuous liberalisation of trade in textiles has considerably affected the European textiles sector. From 1995 to 2005, employment levels in the sector in the EU25 countries decreased by one million to 2.7 million workers and further job losses are anticipated in the years to come, according to a report by the Institute of Manufacturing of the University of Cambridge in 2006.

With the European integration process, the EU has welcomed 12 new Member States since May 2004, bringing the total number of Member States to 27. The group of candidate countries currently includes Croatia, Turkey and the former Yugoslav Republic of Macedonia, while other Western Balkan countries such as Albania, Bosnia and Herzegovina, Montenegro and Serbia including Kosovo are potential candidate countries. The enlargement process and the gradual building up of the internal market is increasing competition in the sector and providing an opportunity for retailers to source manufacturing activities to low-wage countries in central and eastern Europe. The new Member States also represent interesting markets for textiles companies.

In the 1995 Barcelona Declaration, the Euro-Mediterranean Partners agreed on the establishment of a Euro-Mediterranean Free Trade Area (EMFTA) 3 by the target date of 2010. This free trade area is to be achieved by means of the Euro-Mediterranean Association Agreements negotiated and concluded between the European Union and the Mediterranean partners, together with free trade agreements between the partners themselves. Together with the European Free Trade Association (EFTA) comprising Iceland, Liechtenstein, Norway and Switzerland, the free trade zone will include some 40 countries and between 600 and 800 million consumers. It will thus become one of the world's most important trade entities.On 3 October 2003, in Rome, under the Barcelona process, the Mediterranean partners and the European Commission approved the creation of a dialogue group on industrial policy and cooperation. The purpose of this dialogue was to encourage and facilitate exchanges of experience and good practices between both sides of the Mediterranean. In view of the textiles sector's economic significance in the area, the progress and outcome of this dialogue is particularly important for the sector. The objective of the dialogue on the future of the textiles sector in the Euro-Mediterranean area is to foster exchange regarding industrial strategies, with a view to promoting the competitiveness of the textiles sector in the area by policies on education, R&D and technological innovation. Another aim of the dialogue is to encourage and facilitate exchanges of experiences and good practices (European Commission, 2006).

New international standards and regulatory issues are likely to affect the development of the textiles sector in the future. The main areas where new regulation has been or will be introduced include consumer protection, labelling, environmental protection, use of chemicals such as the European Community's REACH regulation, and health and safety in the production of textiles. One of the main threats to growth and innovation in the textiles sector relates to the illegal copying of products. Innovation and creation are key to a sustainable existence and success of the industry. Therefore, it is vital for the industry that IPRs are protected in the global market. This is a major challenge for

SMEs in the sector, as they often lack the necessary resources to protect themselves; for instance, SMEs do not have the financial resources to legally pursue counterfeiters. As a result, counterfeiters have free rein over SMEs' intellectual property. In recent years, the interest in public health and consumer protection has been growing in the textiles sector. Textiles manufacturers have responded to the pressures for enhanced consumer protection with increased scrutiny of the chemicals that they use in their products.

Textiles do not fall under the framework of specific sectoral EU programmes, but they can benefit from numerous horizontal funding programmes at European level. These include the structural funds, the globalisation adjustment fund and the Competitiveness and Innovation Programme (CIP). The European Commission's Framework Programmes for Research also provide an opportunity for companies in the sector to strengthen their competitiveness.

According to the European Central Bank (ECB), global economic activity remains resilient, supported in particular by robust economic growth in emerging economies. Consumer price inflation eased in industrialised countries and cost inflationary pressures recently diminished. However, the recent rise in oil and commodity prices signals a possible renewed increase in global inflationary pressures in the near future. Key risks to future economic growth include the potential for a broader impact from the ongoing reappraisal of risk in financial markets, concerns about protectionist pressures and possible disorderly developments owing to global imbalances, as well as further increases in oil and commodity prices.

Growth in Europe is currently characterised as 'robust', although inflationary developments differ in the European Member States. A range of countries outside the EU have experienced tremendous growth rates, and these countries constitute major market opportunities for high-value added products. In Asia, particularly in China, economic activity continues to expand at a rapid pace. In Latin America, economic activity remains sustained, albeit with some heterogeneity in the growth and inflation performances of major economies (ECB, 2007). Economic growth and an increased purchasing power of people in countries outside the EU constitute a growth opportunity for European companies. However, global expansion is very challenging for many companies – not least for SMEs.

Several aspects such as trade liberalisation, an increasing international division of labour and the resulting 'fragmentation of production' are leading to considerable changes in the value chain of the textiles sector (Jones and Kierzkowski, 2001; Jones et al, 2005), as has already been witnessed over the past decades. Production is increasingly split into separate fragments and generally located in areas where a comparative advantage exists for companies. Different elements of the value chain are currently located in different regions within and outside the EU25: basic manufacturing processes are increasingly based in China, India and other developing countries, while the completion of textile products takes place in several countries of the EU25 and increasingly in the new Member States. The design, research and development (R&D), and innovation in relation to textiles occur to a great extent in relatively high-wage and high-cost regions and locations showing a high level of human capital.

The globalisation of the value chain requires improved communication and better coordination between the different parts of the value chain, thus driving stakeholders' efforts in terms of a horizontal integration in the value chain (EMCC, 2008). The globalisation of the supply chain also entails certain risks for companies in the sector, as they are required to monitor working conditions and manufacturing practices in all parts of the value chain, including those at subcontracting companies. If a company or its subcontractors are not complying with regulation or ethical standards, the image of the company can be damaged. A recent example of a company which faced criticism due to problems in the supply chain is the high street fashion retailer Gap. The company has a factory-monitoring programme and a clear policy on child labour, stating that if Gap discovers that a contractor uses children to manufacture its clothes, the contractor must remove the child from the workplace, provide it with access to schooling and a wage, and guarantee the opportunity of work on reaching a legal working age. All of Gap's suppliers and their subcontractors are required to guarantee that they will not use child labour to produce garments. In recent years, Gap has made efforts to rebrand itself as a leader in ethical and socially responsible manufacturing, after previously being criticised for practices including the use of child labour. Despite its policy on child labour, in October 2007, the company once more had to face severe criticism as a sweatshop was revealed in India where 10-year old children produced Gap garments under slave-like conditions (The Observer, 28 October 2007).

Manufacturing and services have been 'the usual suspects' when it comes to outsourcing of activities. However, high-skilled business functions like R&D seem no longer protected from being outsourced and offshored. This trend has contributed to concerns about the future of the domestic knowledge base in the EU and the resulting impact on competitiveness, notwithstanding the fact that increased international R&D links can promote faster technological change and a broader diffusion of technological advances worldwide. While most R&D internationalisation takes place within the OECD area, developing countries are increasingly attracting R&D centres, although these remain relatively small in a global perspective. Significant increases in foreign R&D investment in Asia, particularly in China and India, have attracted much attention in recent years. It can be expected that this shift will continue to some extent as these countries offer a combination of relatively low wages with a good education system, resulting in a large pool of well-trained researchers (OECD, 2007).

The textiles and clothing sector is subjected to increasing competition from countries outside the EU, especially in labour-intensive activities such as manufacturing of clothes. In such activities, countries in Africa, Asia and Latin America are able to offer very low unit prices. Competition from countries outside the EU is not limited to lower technology industries, but also include more and more high-technology industries. China in particular is moving up the value chain, and even though China's trade surplus is still due to low-technology and labour-intensive industries such as toys, textiles and footwear, the country is developing its own technological capabilities. It has recently implemented a new policy which emphasises the development of domestic innovative capability. This has led to increased spending on R&D and a growing researcher base (OECD, ibid). An increase in the technological and innovative capability in China will increase competition in high-value added products and poses a serious threat to the future market position of European textiles companies.

More and more Indian countries are looking to acquire units in countries which will improve their margins and give them greater access to international markets. One such example is the purchase of the American textiles company Dan River by Indian-based Gujarat Heavy Chemicals (GHCL) in 2006. GHCL bought Dan River for $17.5 million and assumed its $80 million debt. After GHCL had taken over Dan River, it announced that it planned to close the company's manufacturing operations in the US which resulted in the lay off of more than 500 workers. At that time, Dan River already outsourced more than 50 per cent of its manufacturing, much of it to China, India and Pakistan (News-record.com, 14 January 2006). Countries that have been considered sourcing destinations for the manufacturing of textiles have started to set up manufacturing operations in countries such as Africa and China. In 2004, the Indian-based JCT set up a unit in Senegal, as the African Growth and Opportunity Act provides concessions for exports to the EU and the US. Other Indian companies, such as Eskay K'nit and Sabare International, are also starting operations in China (*Textile intelligence*, 18 January 2006).

Women's clothing still accounts for the greatest share of the fashion market. However, as fashion consciousness increases, the menswear and children's wear subsectors are also expanding. This is partially due to the fact that the media is beginning to focus on these groups. Moreover, the market for niche clothing, such as clubwear and surfwear, for example, is also likely to continue expanding. Sportswear is also booming, not just through global manufacturers such as Nike and Adidas, but also through retailers. Meanwhile, the interest in 'eco-friendly' clothing seems to grow as well (AGCAS, Spring 2006). In terms of global markets, the industry is concerned about market liberalisation in Asia. Regarding import tariffs for textiles, there is a need for a reciprocal liberalisation of the markets in Asia. Given import tariffs of 30 per cent or more in Asia, they are still well above EU levels which are, on average, less than 10 per cent. There is also a need for a faster dismantling of non-tariff trade restrictions in Asia. Such a move should significantly improve

European companies' sales prospects in Asia. European clothing labels have a strong reputation in these markets and the share of the population in Asia who can afford and wants upmarket European fashion is on the rise (Heyman, 13 July 2005).

Globalisation and technological progress have led to a rethinking of the textiles industry's clustering strategy. While still playing an important role for some activities, cooperation at local, district or regional level has increasingly proved inadequate to ensure that the chain of production remains at close geographical proximity to the European market. Therefore, clustering of the sector's highly diversified activities is now based on a wider geographical area, such as the Euro-Mediterranean zone (European Commission, February 2005).

China and India are engaging Europe not in a race to the bottom, but also in a race to the top – where the goal is to become the fastest adopters of innovative technology and processes (Ederer et al, 2007). Innovation is vital for the future prospects of the European textiles sector. It can be driven by technological developments and/or new creative designs, and result in new products with a range of functionalities, also enhancing the quality of life. Innovation in the production process can contribute to raising the sector's productivity, improving working conditions and promoting sustainable manufacturing. In the clothing industry, new technologies will enable the EU industry to offer products tailored to the individual needs and wishes of a customer, while being manufactured

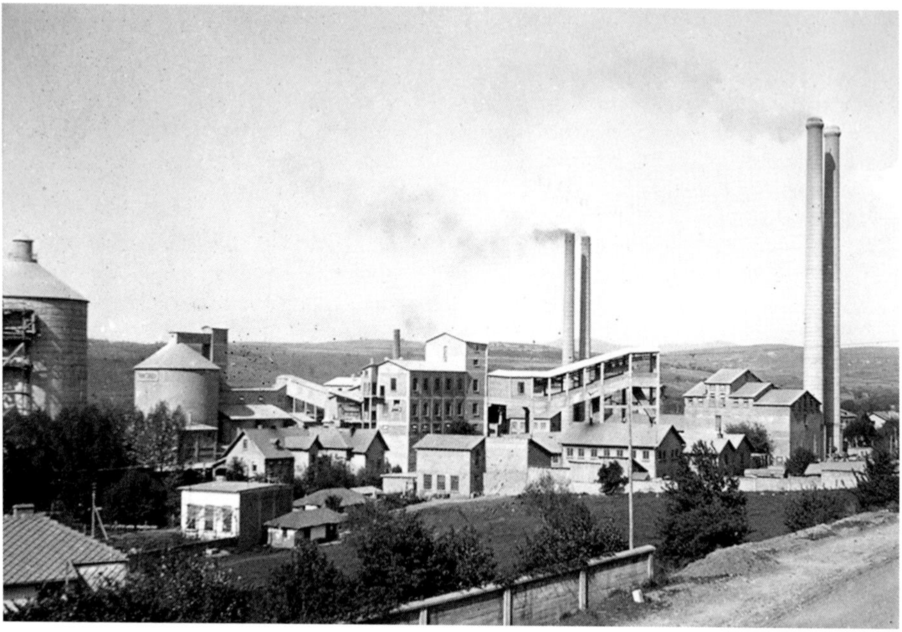

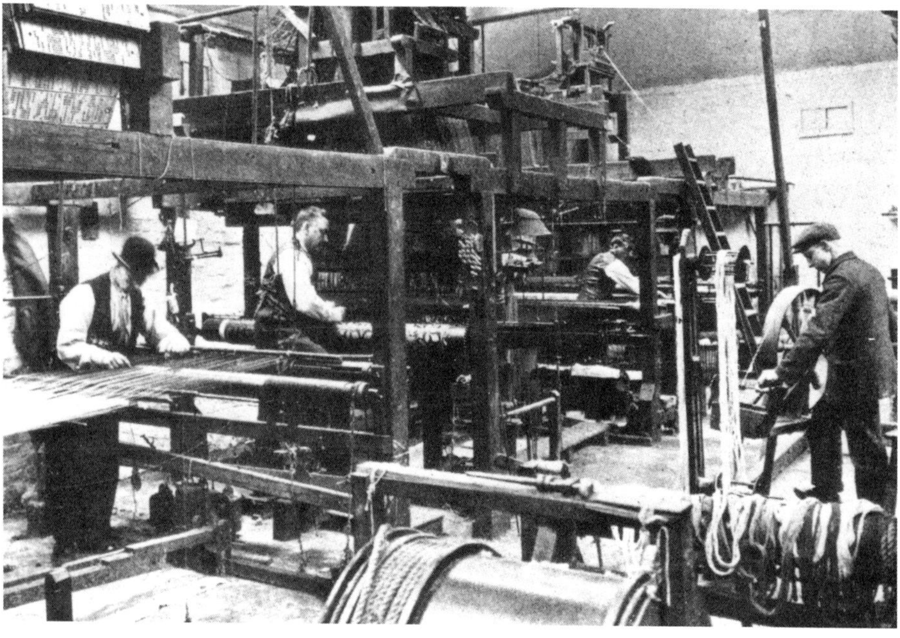

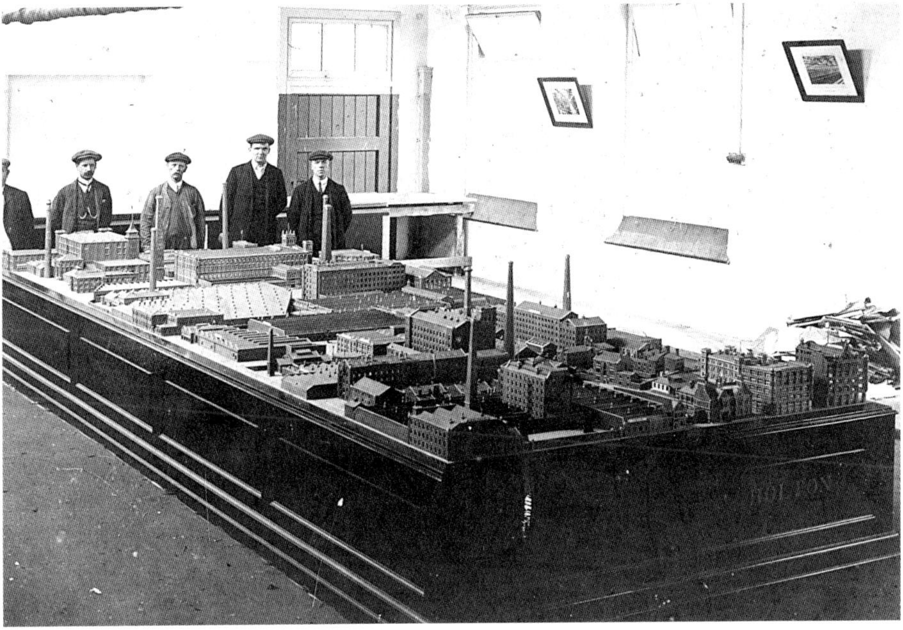

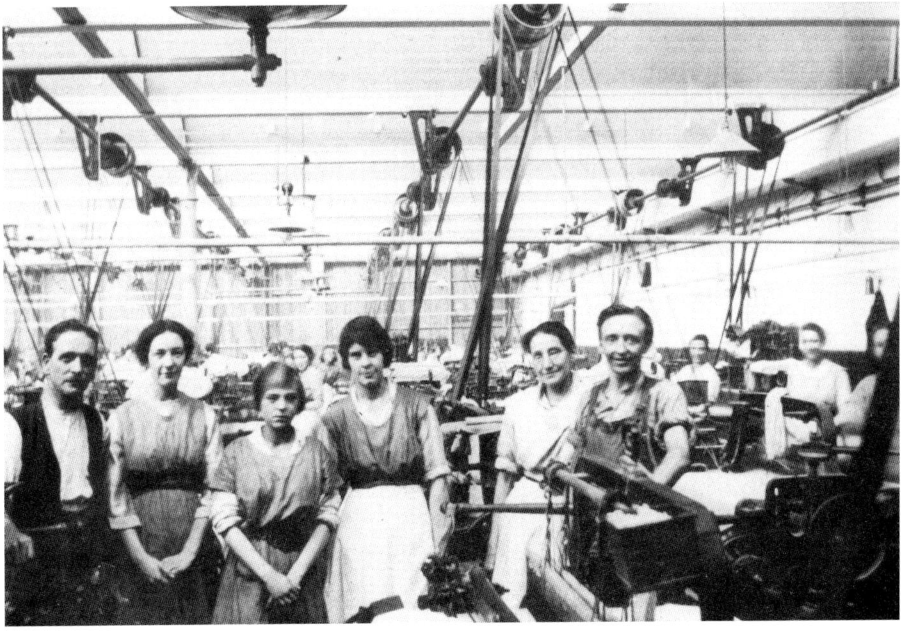

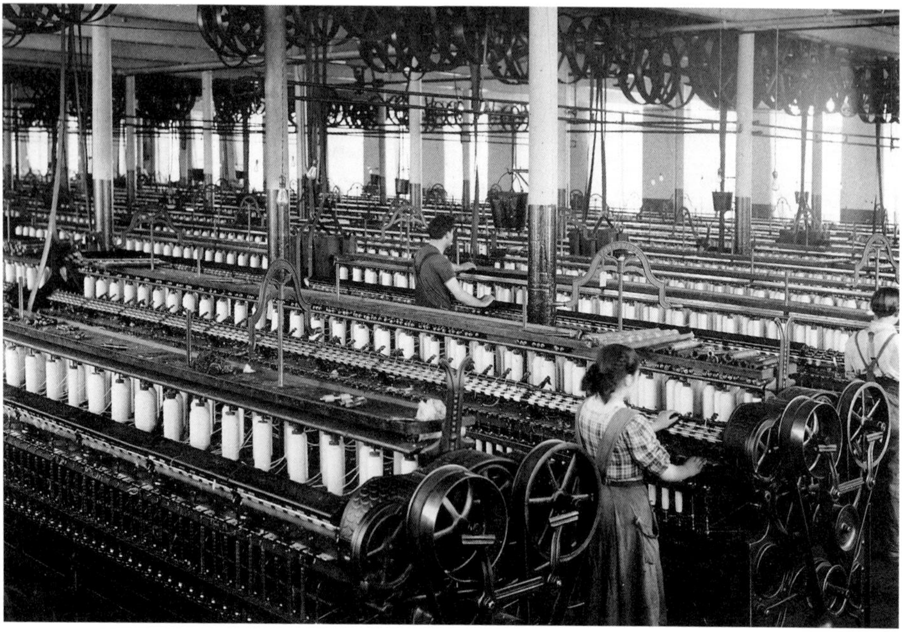

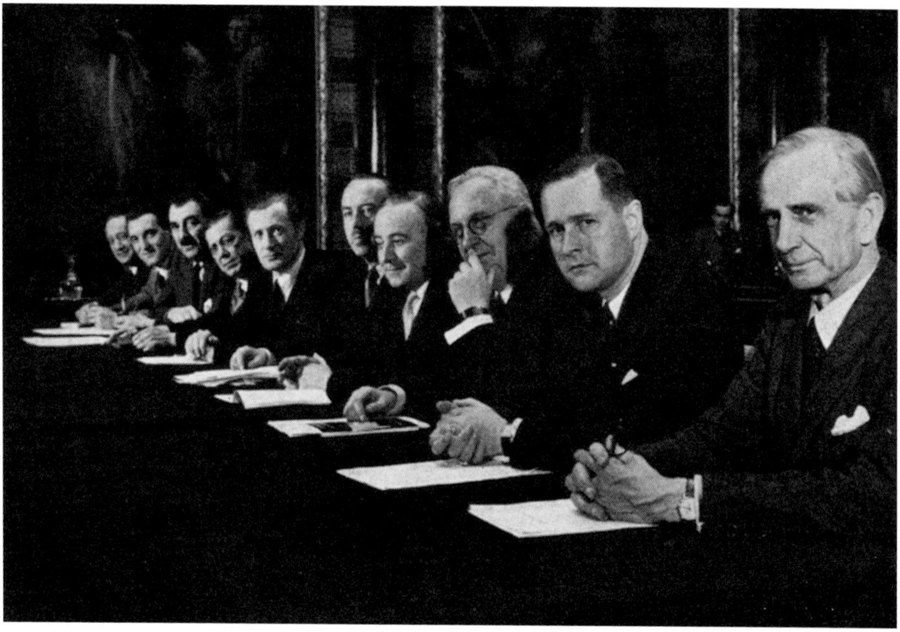

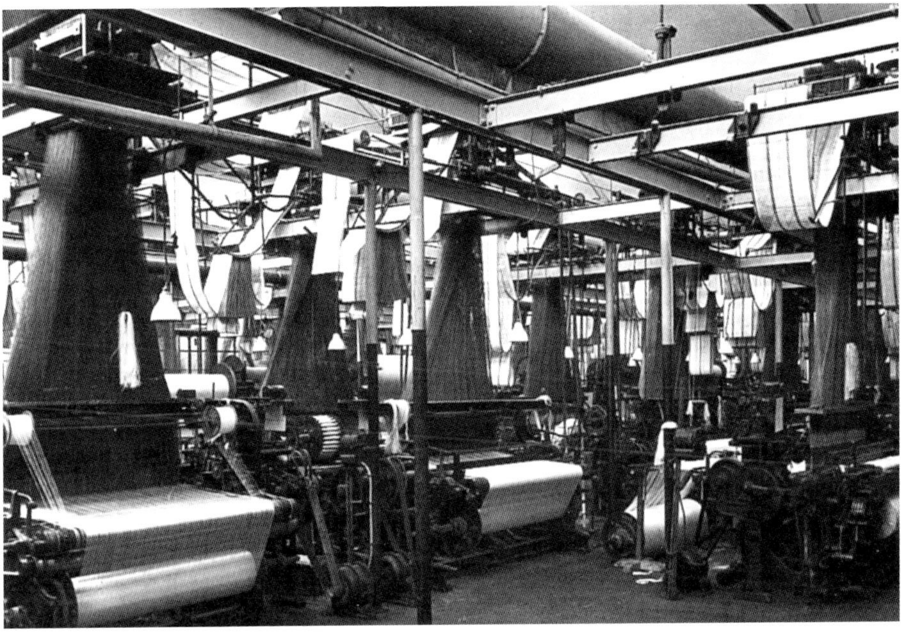

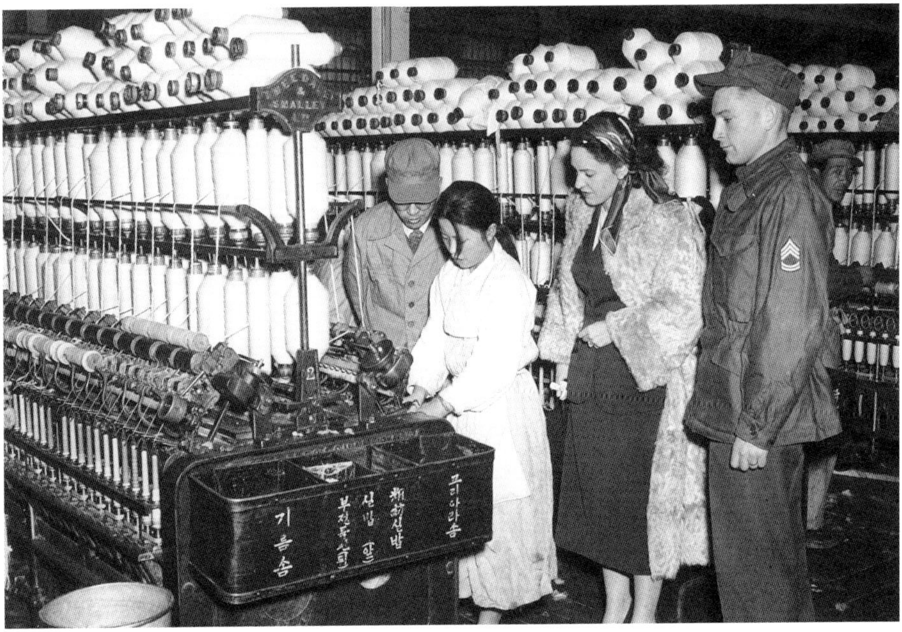

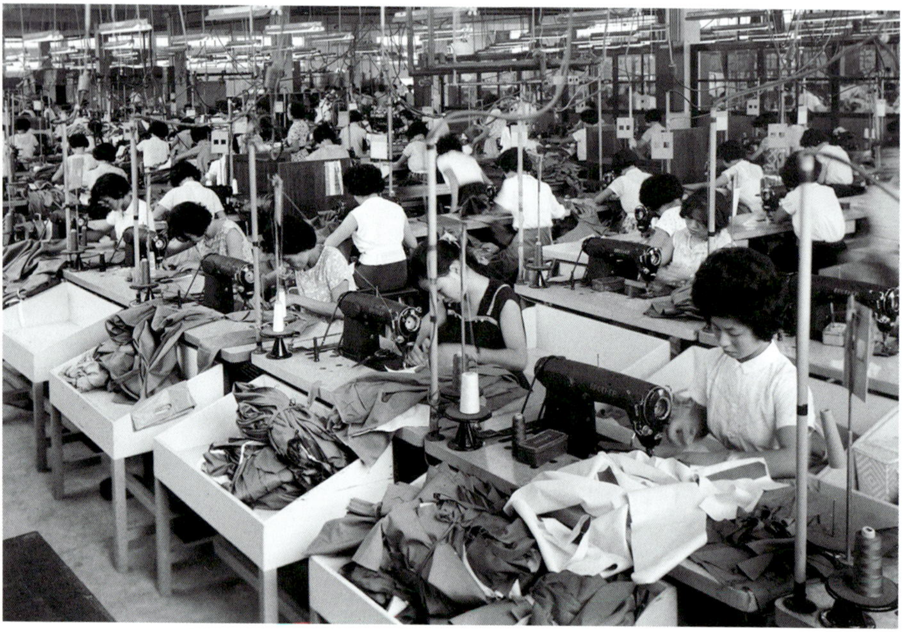

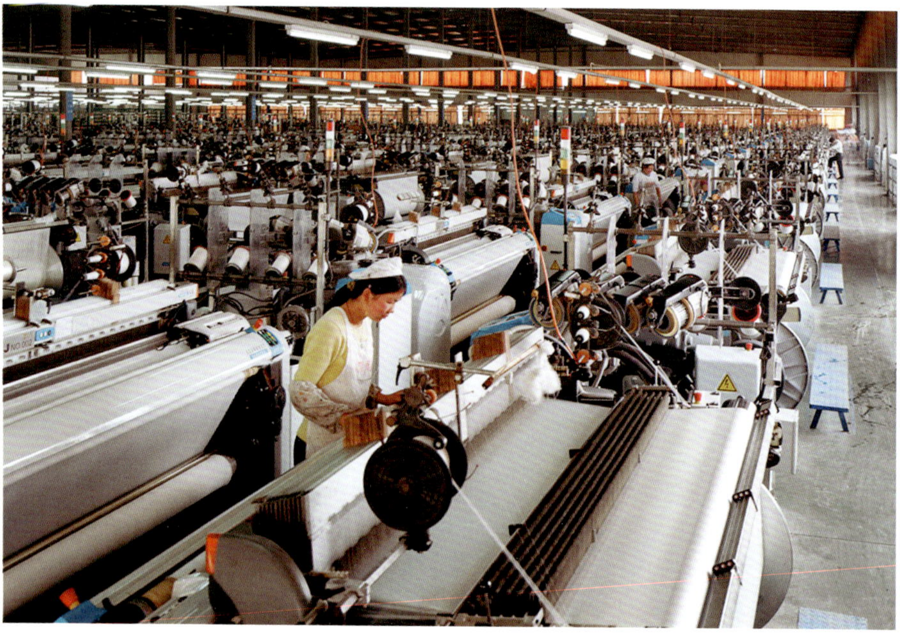

18
The first Bulgarian factory
for textiles was opened in
Sliven, 1836

The Weaving Shed at
Merton Abbey in the parish
of Merton in London, 1890

19
Horrockses Yard Works mill
model made by Horrockses
employees for the occasion
of the Royal Visit to Preston
Harris Museum & Art
Gallery, 1913

Weavers at the Horrockses
factory Preston. This is the
location where the Preston
Guild cotton arch was built,
commemorating the Town's
textile trades, 1917

20
Three spinners in spinning
room, 1919

Robert Bichet with other
members of the European
Movement at the Brussels
Conference, 1949

21
Elias textile factory
Eindhoven employed 200
workers, 1950

Chinese textile factory
during the Communist
regime, 1950

22
During the 1960s and
1970s textile was one of
Taiwan's key export
industries, 1964

Chinese textile plant,1998

in a mass-production system. Such mass-customisation, facilitating the production of tailor-made clothing at cheap prices, will provide the EU industry with a competitive advantage over mass-produced clothing.

The European textiles and clothing industry was one of the first sectors to establish social dialogue at the European level. Today, the sectoral social dialogue committee for textiles and clothing meets about every four to six months to discuss ongoing issues. The topics discussed mainly concern the modernisation of work organisation, anticipation of structural changes and measures to accompany restructuring processes, adaptation of the contractual framework that allows the development of new employment forms, and access to training. The two main organisations in the textiles and clothing sector — namely, ETUF:TCL and Euratex — have been working together in an informal way since 1992. At present, both organisations participate in the European sectoral social dialogue committee for the textiles and clothing sector which was established in 1999. As already mentioned, one of the main achievements of the EU sectoral social dialogue in the textiles and clothing sector is the creation of a code of conduct in 1997, in which the social partners call on their members to actively encourage companies and workers in their sector to comply with the ILO conventions in relation to core labour standards.

Activities in the EU sectoral social dialogue committee currently focus on vocational training, enlargement and restructuring. The committee also discusses industrial and social measures with the aim of improving the competitiveness of the sector while emphasising the implementation of the recommendations of the High Level Group as a follow-up to the Commission's Communication on The future of the textiles and clothing sector in the enlarged European Union(European Commission, 2003). Furthermore, as mentioned earlier, the social partners plan the creation of a European observatory for training and employment, including the setting up of an information and media pool aimed at the development of educational material for teachers and common qualification standards. The aim of such an information pool is to facilitate mobility between countries, improve the image of the sector and attract young people to work in the sector (European Commission, 2006).

A key restructuring issue is the particular situation of SMEs in the sector. While the closure of large companies in the sector will often attract a lot of attention and spur actions which aim to counter the negative effects of such closures, the closure of small enterprises will most often remain unnoticed and not lead to any initiatives to deal with the knock-on effects. Moreover, the closure of large companies will affect many subcontractors which are not necessarily part of a scheme aimed at supporting the restructuring process. As a result, a lot of small companies in the sector and in local communities will slowly disappear over time and redundant workers will often have to cope with the situation on their own without any specific schemes set up to help them to find other employment opportunities. Some workers who lose their jobs may have to live without a salary for several weeks or months while trying to find new jobs. In addition, depending on their skills and experience, they may have to accept jobs at lower salaries. The mere threat of moving production facilities overseas is often used as a means of keeping wages low and reducing workers' health insurance and pension benefits (OECD, 2004). In fact, whole districts with a predominant activity in the textiles sector and consisting mainly of SMEs are at risk of disappearing without any type of measures in place which aim to support a sustainable transformation of the area. The workers left behind, as well as whole communities, may experience a particularly difficult time due to the negative socioeconomic effects of restructuring.

Many companies and trade unions in the new Member States do not have sufficient experience with social dialogue. Hence, there is a need to build capacity for social dialogue and managing restructuring processes in these countries. The capacity-building initiatives in Bulgaria launched by the Italian-based Miroglio Group constitute a good example of how companies in the sector can contribute to the positive development in this area. Like most large groups in the textiles and clothing sector, the Miroglio Group has engaged in the restructuring of production units that are unable to outperform those located in the Asian economies. When the group had to close down manufacturing sites in Italy and Germany, company management began negotiations with workers' representatives in an attempt to find mutually acceptable social solutions. Such negotiations, however, did not

take place in Bulgaria where several of the group's production units which were also facing restructuring are located. This led the Miroglio Group to launch a training programme for the management and staff representatives of its Bulgarian undertakings which covered all aspects of their social responsibilities. One of the training programme's outcomes was the negotiation of a collective agreement on trade union consultation and involvement in 2001. The agreement set out the trade unions' role in the management of problems related to issues such as flexibility, productivity or restructuring. Since then, the Miroglio Group has organised a series of training courses for the Bulgarian trade union representatives, including a course module on the 'Right to information and consultation: knowledge is for sharing' and the 'Right to information and consultation in the restructuring processes of multinational companies'. These training programmes were financed by the European Commission and implemented in partnership with Euratex, ETUF-TCL and the Association of Bulgarian Industries. The project was also subsidised by Bulgaria's Ministry of Labour and Social Policy, its federation of light industries which is affiliated to Bulgaria's Confederation of Independent Unions and the 'Podkrepa' Confederation of Labour (MIRE, 2007).

In 2003, the Tuscan regional government launched a three-year integrated pilot project in the areas of textiles, clothing, shoes, leather and jewellery. This initiative sought to strengthen the competitiveness of SMEs in the fashion field, by supporting innovation, as well as the organisational and financial strength of these companies. The initiative was based on a strategic regional plan and involved business associations, trade unions, local government and chambers of commerce.

Nine Spanish regions followed the Italian example and elaborated strategic plans providing for territorial and sectoral policy tools. The Spanish members of the Association of European Textile Collectivities (ACTE) and representatives of the Spanish Textiles Council (Consejo Intertextil Espagnol) participated in the project, which was completed in June 2005. The project has resulted in various specific initiatives across these regions, notably: the Integrated Services for Textiles (SIT) of the Mataro City Council facilitating the relocation of textiles workers and occupational training; a project entitled 'Strategic vision for the textiles cluster Sabadell and Terrassa' promoting collaboration in the textiles sector and with the aeronautics and railways sectors to produce high value-added products; the establishment of the Anoia Textile Observatory; and the support plan for the textiles and clothing sector initiated by the Spanish Ministry of Employment and Industry (High Level Group for textiles and clothing, 2006).

Another good example of how to successfully manage restructuring processes is the transformation of the textiles and clothing sector in the province of Łódź in central Poland. The city of Łódź has been dependent on its textiles industry for more than 1,500 years. During the former communist regime, some 60% of all textiles employees in Poland worked in the province of Łódź and produced about 40 per cent of the national manufacture of cotton and silk fabrics, and 33 per cent of wool fabrics. However, when the Soviet Union collapsed and the sector was suddenly exposed to international competition, the industry as well as the whole community faced a major challenge with many companies going bankrupt and unemployment rising dramatically. At the beginning of this decade, the unemployment rate in the region stood at about 20 per cent, which affected all aspects of life in the community. The political leadership of the city tackled this challenge by creating investor-friendly conditions and providing incentives for local entrepreneurship. With the assistance of external consultants, politicians developed a business plan for the city of Łódź, identifying three priority branches of economic activity: managing offshoring business processes, logistics and manufacturing of household appliances. The key focus of these three areas of activity is the introduction of new technologies. The objective of this business plan is the creation of 25,000 new jobs by 2010 and 40,000 new jobs by 2015. The implementation of the business plan is already showing some results: the unemployment rate was down to 12 per sent in April 2007 and a range of large companies, including Philips, General Electrics, Polish Telecom, DB Schenker and Dell, have set up business in the city. However, Łódź has not abandoned its textiles and clothing industry, but has instead engaged in a transformation of the industry from a labour-intensive to a research-intensive industry. The initiatives in this respect include the establishment of different research consortia involving the Łódź Technical University with its centre for human-friendly advanced textiles technology

'Pro Humano Tex' and rebuilding bonds between research institutions and entrepreneurs by establishing a Polish Industry Platform. This platform is headquartered at the Department of Textiles Engineering and Marketing of the Łódź Technical University. It supports the development of the Łódź textiles and clothing cluster, as well as cluster-wide initiatives which aim to promote innovation. As a result, the city of Łódź has managed to retain its role as a textiles and clothing producer. A key aspect of the transformation of the Łódź province has been the focus on community development. This process included transforming old buildings into new and interesting places to work and live, engaging in urban development projects and crea-ting a positive and forward-looking culture among the city's inhabitants. The relocation of employees who have been made redundant – either within the same company or to other companies in the area or those located outside the area – constitutes an important element of sustainable approaches to company restructuring.

The restructuring processes of two French-based textiles companies, namely Trèves and Damart, are good company case examples of how to approach restructuring in the sector. In the case of Damart, which mainly serves the market of thermal wear for people aged 50 years and over, the restructuring plan was announced several years before the production unit in question was actually closed down. The group undertook to internally reclassify all shop-floor staff in new jobs, mainly in logistics or sales activities. To trigger motivation for mobility among the older, often poorly-skilled members of staff, for whom reclassification meant going back to study, the company first carried out a test phase among volunteers. About 40 female workers were reclassified in new jobs, which often were different from their previous occupations, following training and a follow-up period enabling them to cope with the demands of the new job. Over 18 months after the reclassification, all remaining 120 staff members were monitored in similar conditions before the workshop was completely closed down. The French textiles group, Trèves, which mainly serves the automotive market, introduced a prevention-based strategy for the company to initiate the forward-looking management of jobs and skills. While the company prepared a restructuring process which was likely to involve the loss of about 800 jobs across several sites over a two-year period, management began a series of negotiations with the company's various trade union federations. A first agreement between the two parties resulted in the creation of a joint working group for the exchange of information and negotiation; the working group comprised representatives of the trade unions and staff of the main sites scheduled for restructuring. The negotiations which took place within the working group resulted in three further agreements outlining the underlying terms and conditions of the restructuring process: one agreement provided for the information and consultation of staff representative bodies of the various companies concerned, a second one for the social measures associated with the restructuring plan and a third for the implementation of the forward-looking management procedures governing employment and skills. All of the trade union federations signed these agreements, the aim of which is to limit the social consequences of restructuring and to safeguard the future of the sites and staff. The observatory has taken steps to carry out a study of workers' abilities, knowledge and trends in the various sector trades. In parallel, programmes for training and the validation of acquired experience have been set up to satisfy two priorities: the development of skills required for the sector's trades and support for possible transfers to trade occupations in other sectors. The skills acquired through the exercise of a textiles or clothing trade are partially transferable and can be put to good use in other trades. Qualifications-based training courses have therefore been designed to develop skills suited to new trade activities in the sector, while certificate courses and VAE activities have been designed to provide interdisciplinary diplomas. The VAE system involves examining the diploma courses available, on which the workers concerned could enrol by taking into account their existing skills. For this purpose, workers can have one or several personal interviews to help them position themselves appropriately and draft their application. Workers may also be tested by an organisation experienced in establishing competence assessments and, if required, any additional course modules will be included to fill in gaps in an applicants' curriculum vitae (CV), thus providing all participants with a good chance of successfully completing the selected course programme.

The Regional plan for textiles and clothing (PRTH) in the Nord Pas-de-Calais region in northern France represented a forward-looking initiative involving public authorities and social partners. The plan was launched at the beginning of the new millennium and specifically addressed the issue of workers' mobility, by preparing employees in textiles and clothing to change jobs either within the sector or move to other sectors of the economy. The plan's primary objective was to monitor industrial change in the sector in that region and, in particular, the monitoring of information and training provided to the sector's workforce. The former translated into the creation of a job and qualifications observatory and the latter into the design and creation of training courses primarily for blue-collar workers, thus leading to qualifications, diplomas and the validation of acquired experience (VAE) schemes. The observatory has taken steps to carry out a study of workers' abilities, knowledge and trends in the various sector trades. In parallel, programmes for training and the validation of acquired experience have been set up to satisfy two priorities: the development of skills required for the sector's trades and support for possible transfers to trade occupations in other sectors.

The involvement of all of the industry's stakeholders – namely, trade unions, employers and public authorities – in restructuring processes is key to ensuring the successful adjustment of the industry to current and future challenges. An interesting, although not sector-specific example, of a national initiative concerns the job security agreements in Sweden. Job security agreements are branch-level agreements initiated by a joint working group and designed to help manage the reclassification of redundant workers. The so-called 'job security foundations' are jointly driven and subsidised by a monthly contribution deducted from workers' salaries and paid by the companies within the relevant branch; if necessary, these contributions are supplemented by public authorities. The job security foundations are organised on a regional basis and offer financial support – particularly in the form of indemnity allowances – and personalised assistance in job seeking. They intervene on the announcement of a restructuring plan. The intervention of the job security foundations is designed to take place in a spirit of cooperation, involving both the employers and trade unions whenever redundancies are scheduled and, subsequently, the department of employment. The workers concerned are individually advised of their redundancy from the moment the restructuring notice is issued and they receive support throughout the notice period – that is, the period preceding the premature termination of their employment contract. Following an initial meeting with their adviser, they are given practical advice in seeking employment or they are directed towards a retraining programme or assisted in setting up their own business. The reclassification results in Sweden are impressive: in general, 70 per cent of a company's workforce are reclassified before the end of the notice period, which usually covers three to 12 months depending on the branch and a worker's length of service, and only 10 per cent of redundant workers would still be jobless after 18 months (MIRE website, 2007). Most OECD countries have already established programmes to deal with the effects of trade liberalisation on national labour markets. Besides unemployment insurance systems, training is probably the second most prevalent aspect of direct or active labour market adjustment programmes in OECD countries. In countries like Germany, providing training to unemployed workers is part of a comprehensive policy in relation to training and vocational programmes. Other countries have implemented a mix of private and public training schemes. Such training programmes fall into two broad categories: providing basic skills in language and mathematics to those with low educational attainment, and providing training in specific job-related skills. Deficiencies in basic skills are particularly common among workers in traditional low-skill manufacturing jobs, for example, in the textiles and clothing industries, where many workers have less than a secondary school education. The lack of basic skills places an added burden on an already difficult adjustment process when such workers face the need to find a new job (OECD, 2004).

Economic fabric, originally published as: Trends and drivers of change in the European textiles and clothing sector: Mapping report

Commissioned by the European Monitoring Centre on Change (EMCC)

© European Foundation for the Improvement of Living and Working Conditions (Eurofound), 2008

The European Flag, an Introduction by the Council of Europe Archives

After its foundation in 1949, the Council of Europe soon realised it needed symbols to show its commitment to European unity. The European Flag and the European Anthem, adopted in 1955 and 1972 respectively, represent a common identity for 800 million Europeans.

The idea for a European flag dates from the early 1920s. The two main forerunners: Count Coudenhove-Kalergi's Pan-European Union flag, a yellow circle with a red cross on a blue background, and the European Movement's green 'E' on a white background. Neither inspired much support and no serious attempt was made to promote the idea of a flag until the Council of Europe became Europe's first official political organisation in 1949.

In 1950, a committee assigned to study the question. Paul MG Levy, the first Director of Press and Information, stressed the need for heraldic assistance in the design. Groups of experts, boards and committees made a lengthy study of over 100 suggestions from artists, heraldry experts and enthusiastic amateurs all over the world. Nothing was decided upon.

In April 1955, the Committee of Ministers chose two designs, one by Arsène Heitz, a member of staff. The first was a crown "of 12 golden stars with 5 rays", their points not touching" and the second, a constellation of stars—originally proposed by Salvador de Madariaga. The Committee of

Ministers preferred the 12 star flag and indicated their preference to the Parliamentary Assembly. In December 1955, the Parliamentary Assembly adopted the 12 star flag "on an azure background with a circle of 12 separate five-pointed gold stars". All European institutions were urged to adopt it. The Committee of Ministers inaugurated it at the Château de la Muette in Paris on 13 December 1955. The flag was now official.

The circle of 12 stars against a blue sky symbolises the peoples of Europe. The circle is the sign of union. The number 12 is the symbol of perfection and entirety. The flag caught the public imagination. Its use at the Universal Exhibition in Brussels in 1958 brought recognition throughout Europe; it flew on public buildings throughout the city.

The advent of an elected European Parliament in 1979 saw the launch of a new initiative to find a European Community flag—and on 28 April 1983 the European Parliament decreed that the Council's flag should be Europe's official emblem. It was adopted by the European Council in Milan on 29 June 1985 and has been used by the European Union since 1986.

Opposite page

The base colour of the flag of Europe is a dark blue called 'reflex blue', a mix of cyan and magenta.

Collection

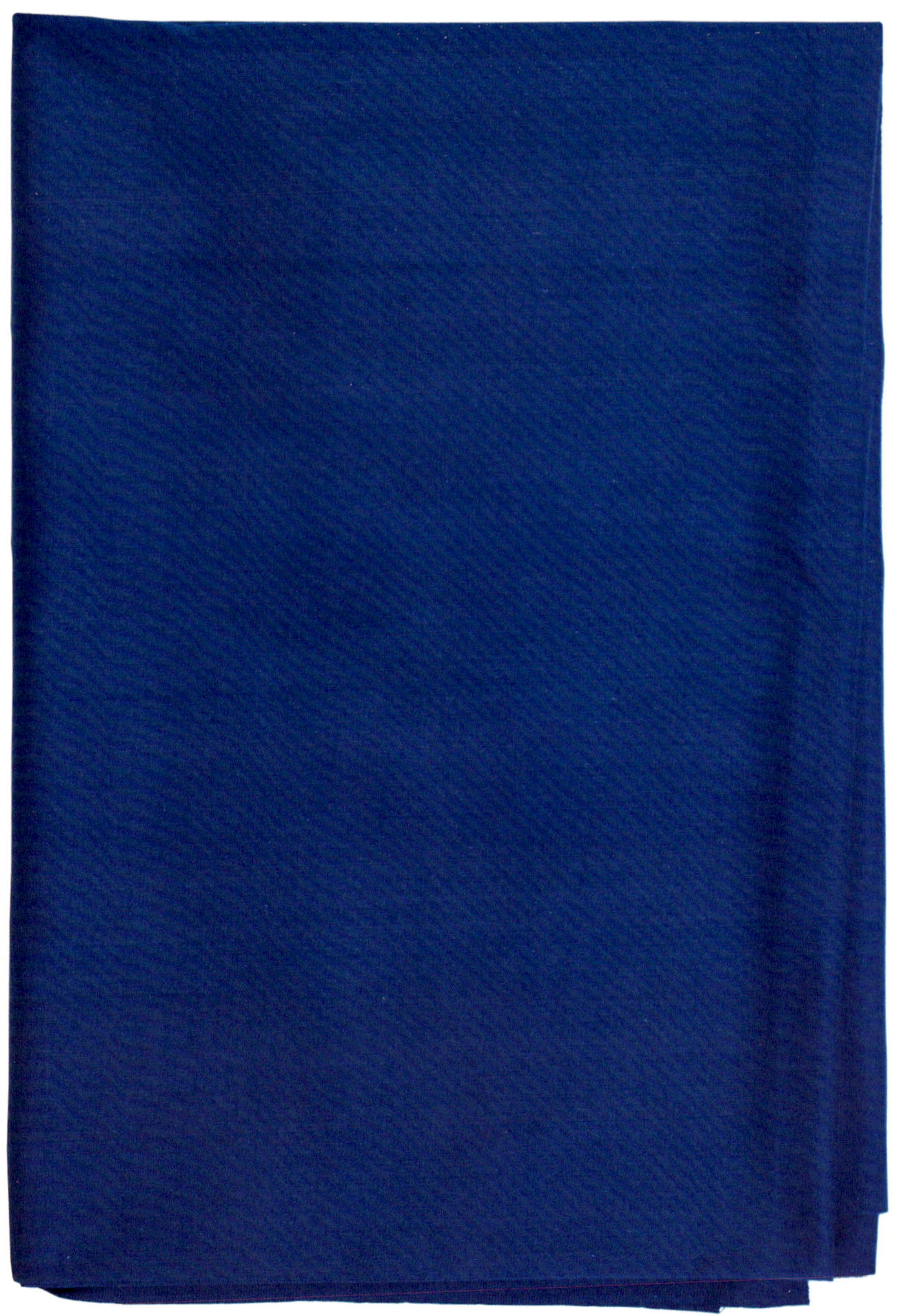

Austria

Belgium

Bulgaria

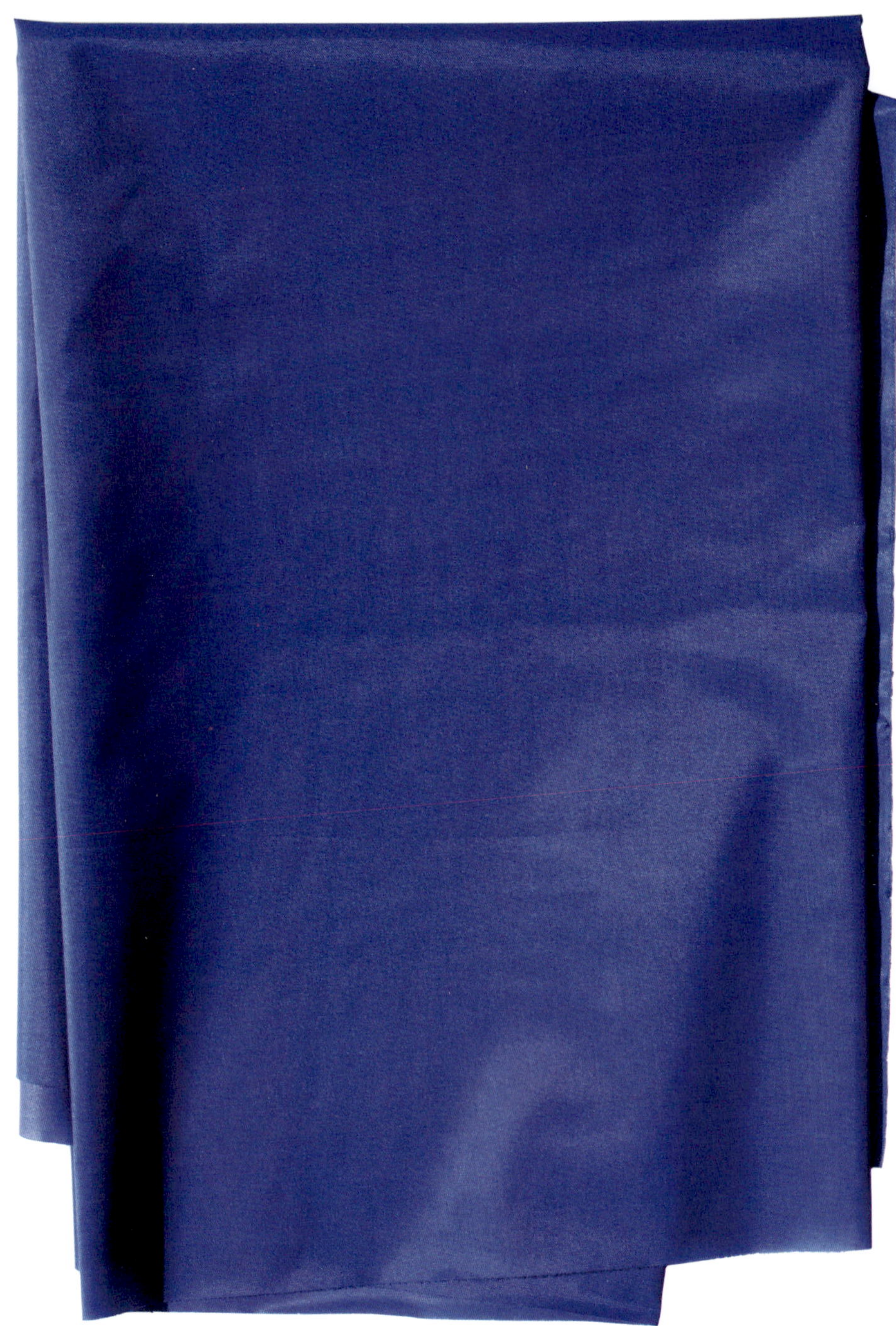

Croatia

Cyprus

Czech Republic

Denmark

Estonia

Finland

France

Germany

Greece

Hungary

Ireland

Italy

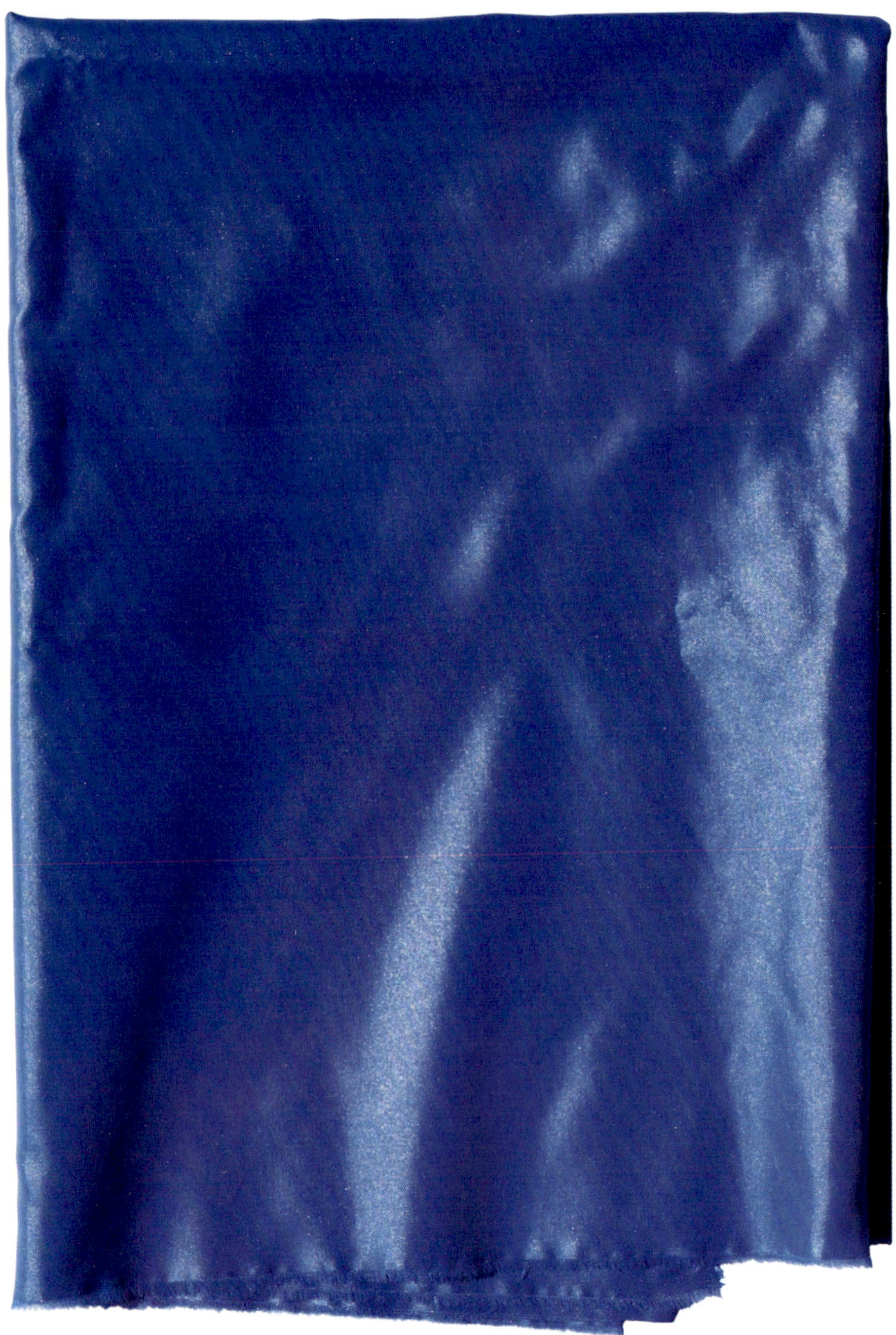

Latvia

Lithuania

Luxembourg

Malta

Netherlands

Poland

Portugal

Romania

Slovakia

Slovenia

Spain

Sweden

United Kingdom

Installation

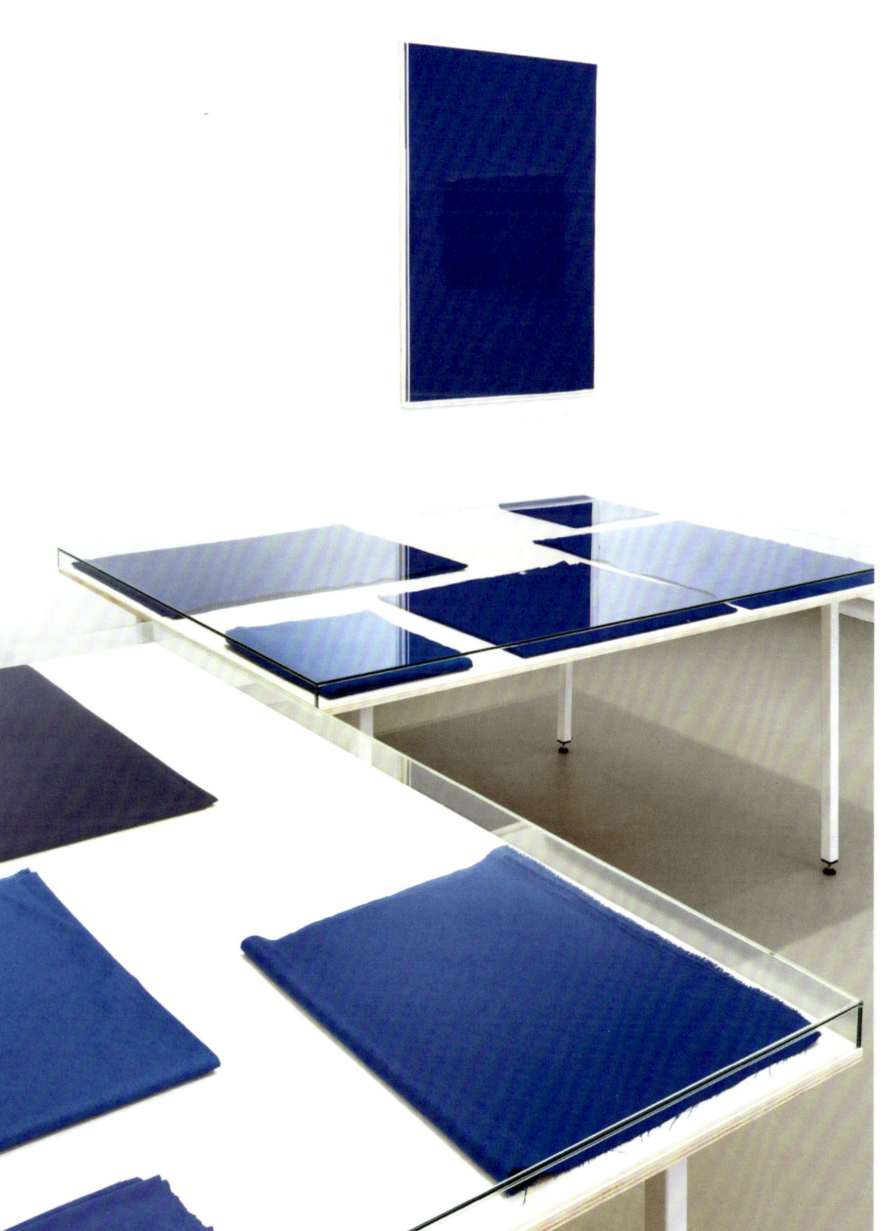

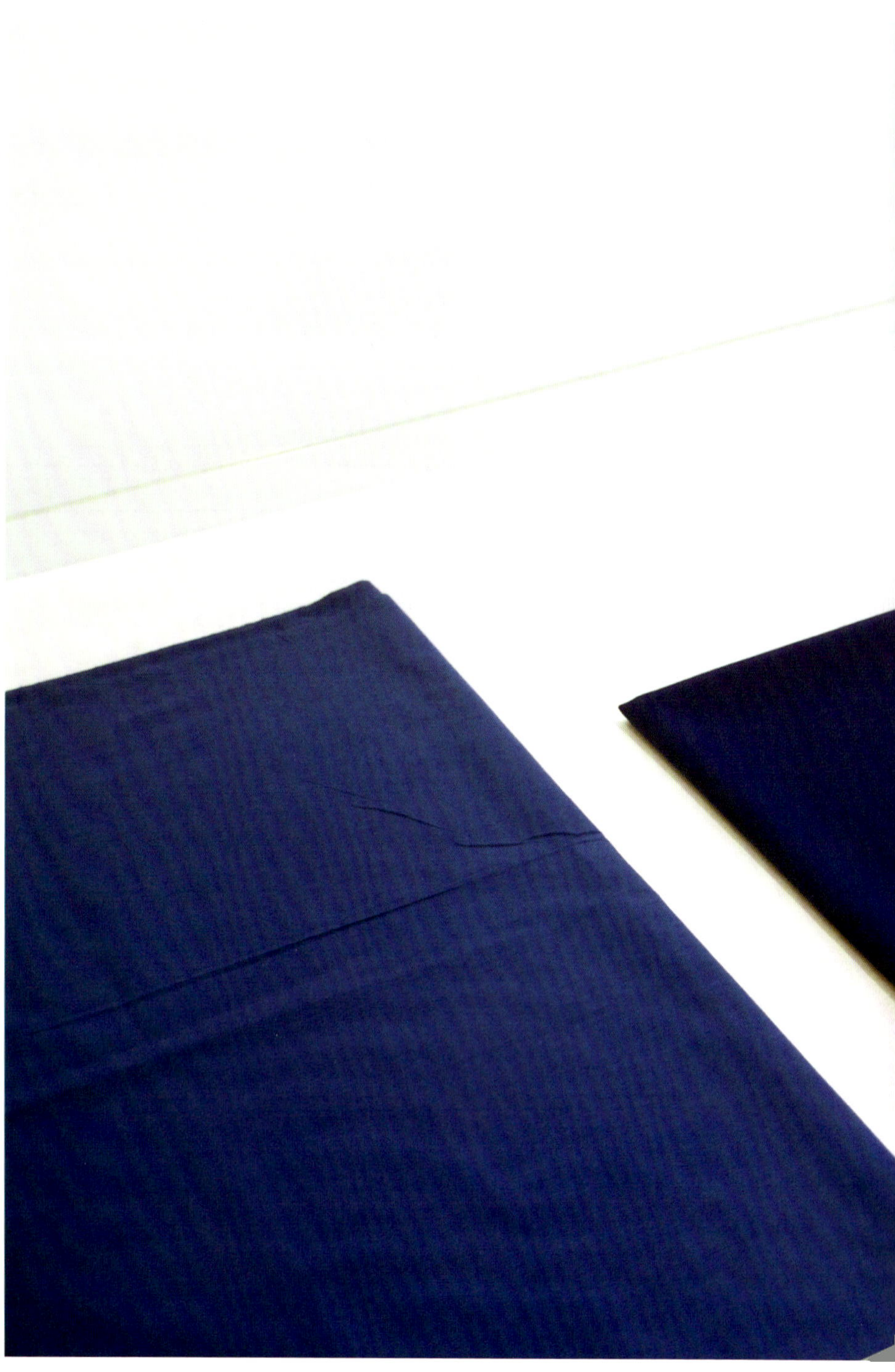

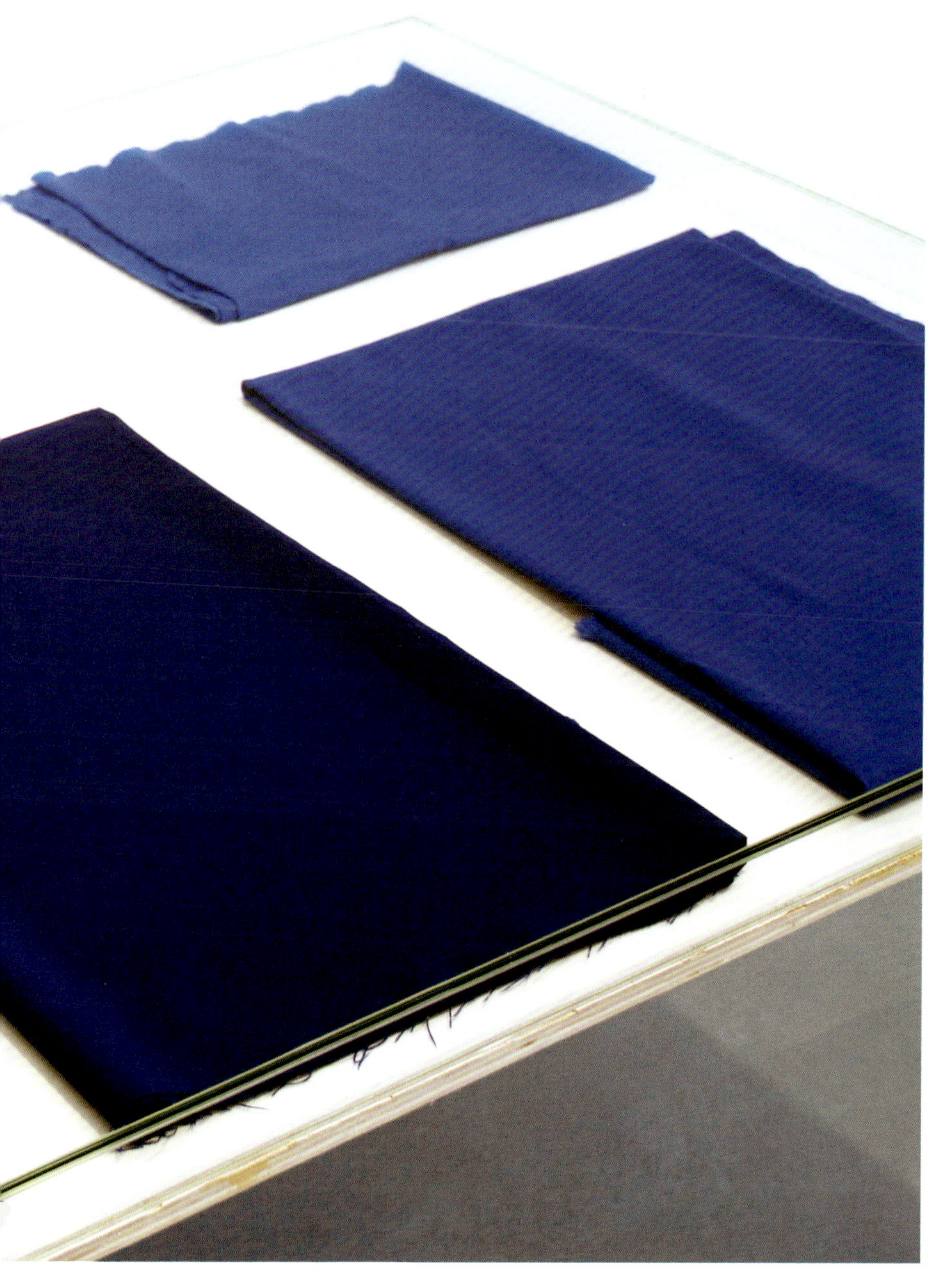

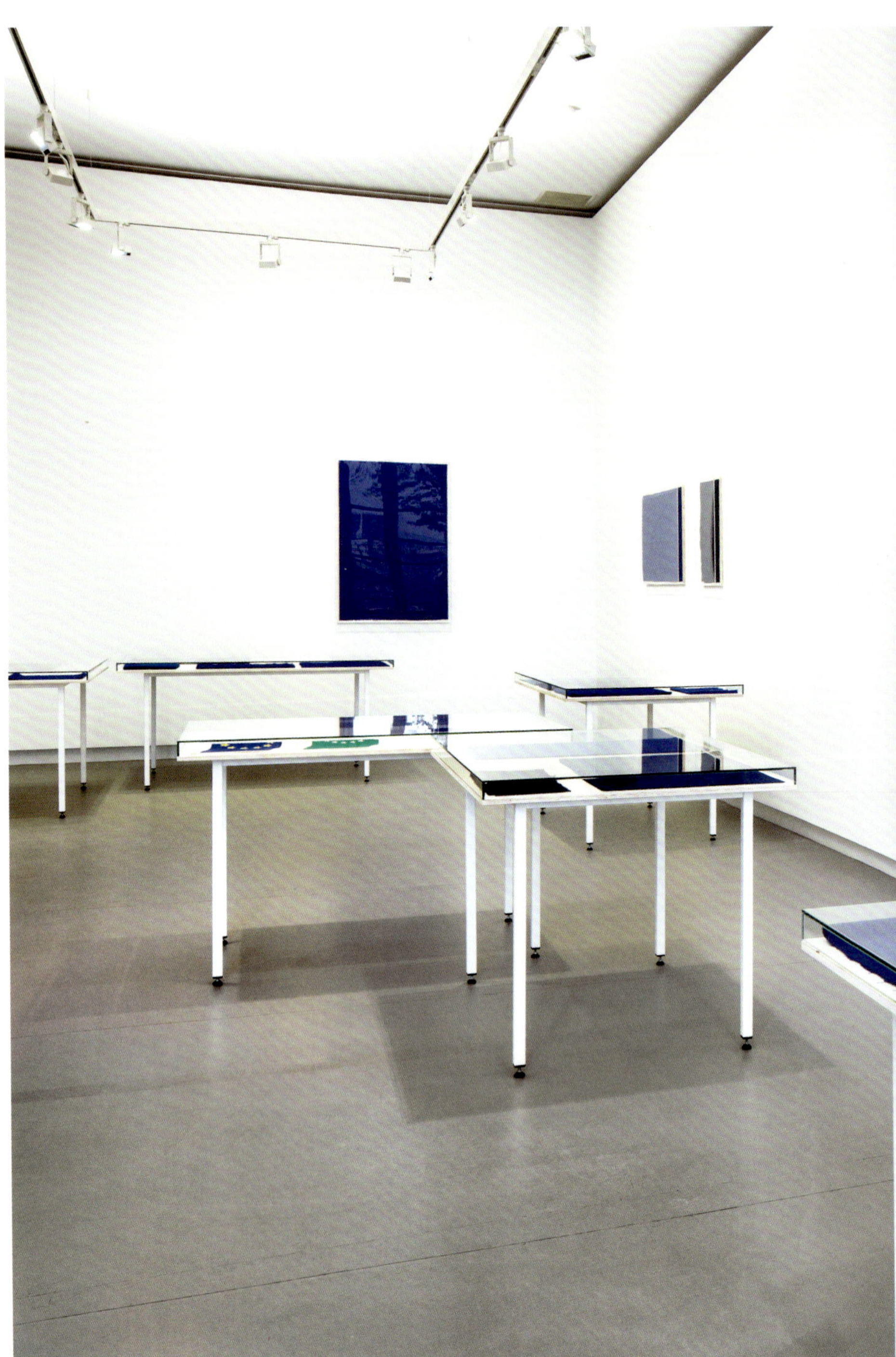

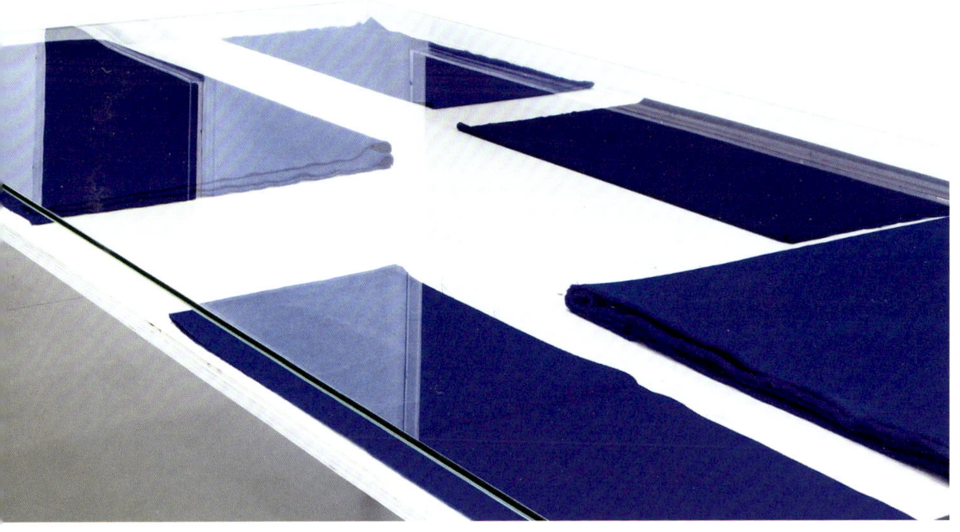

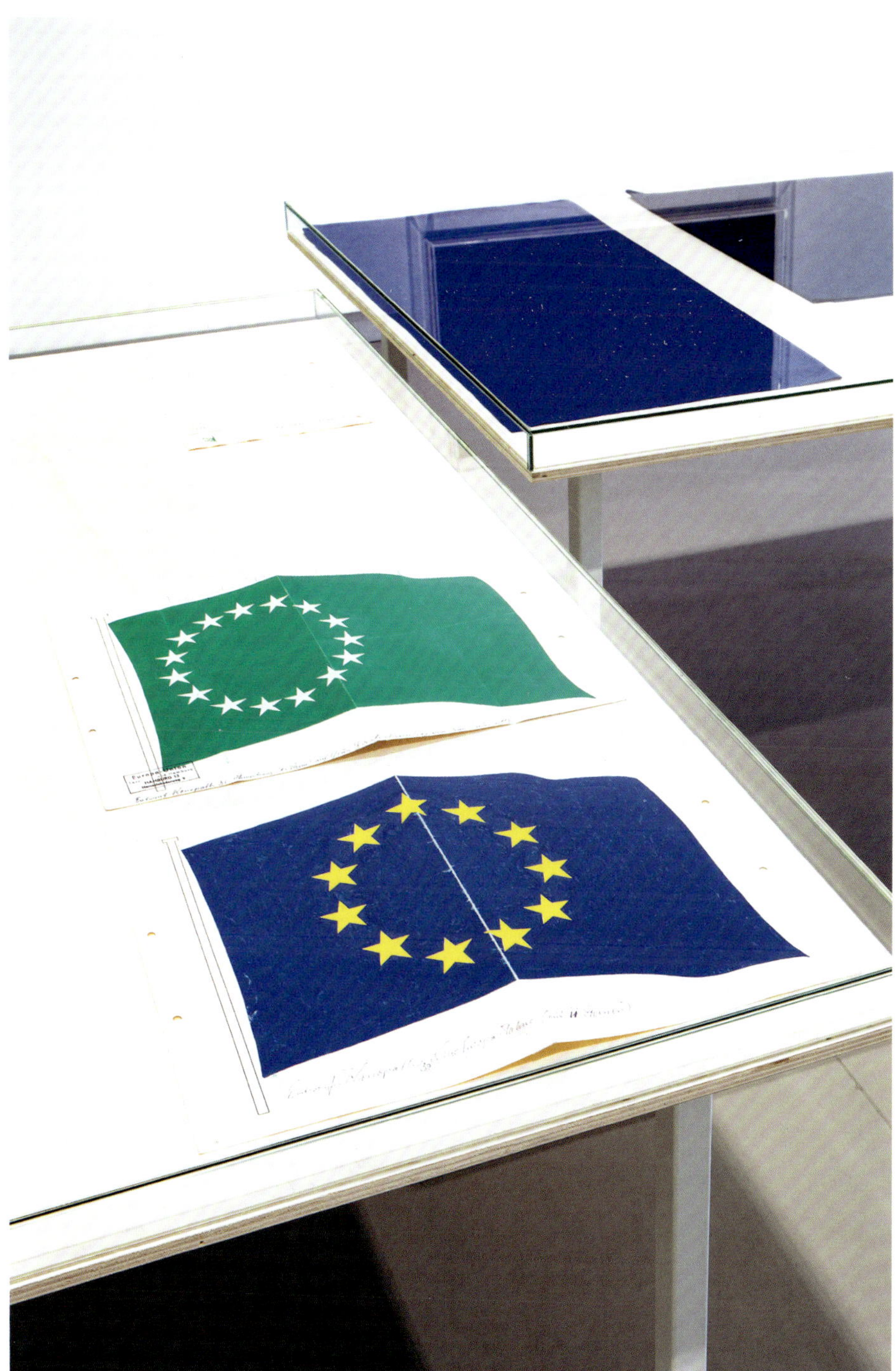

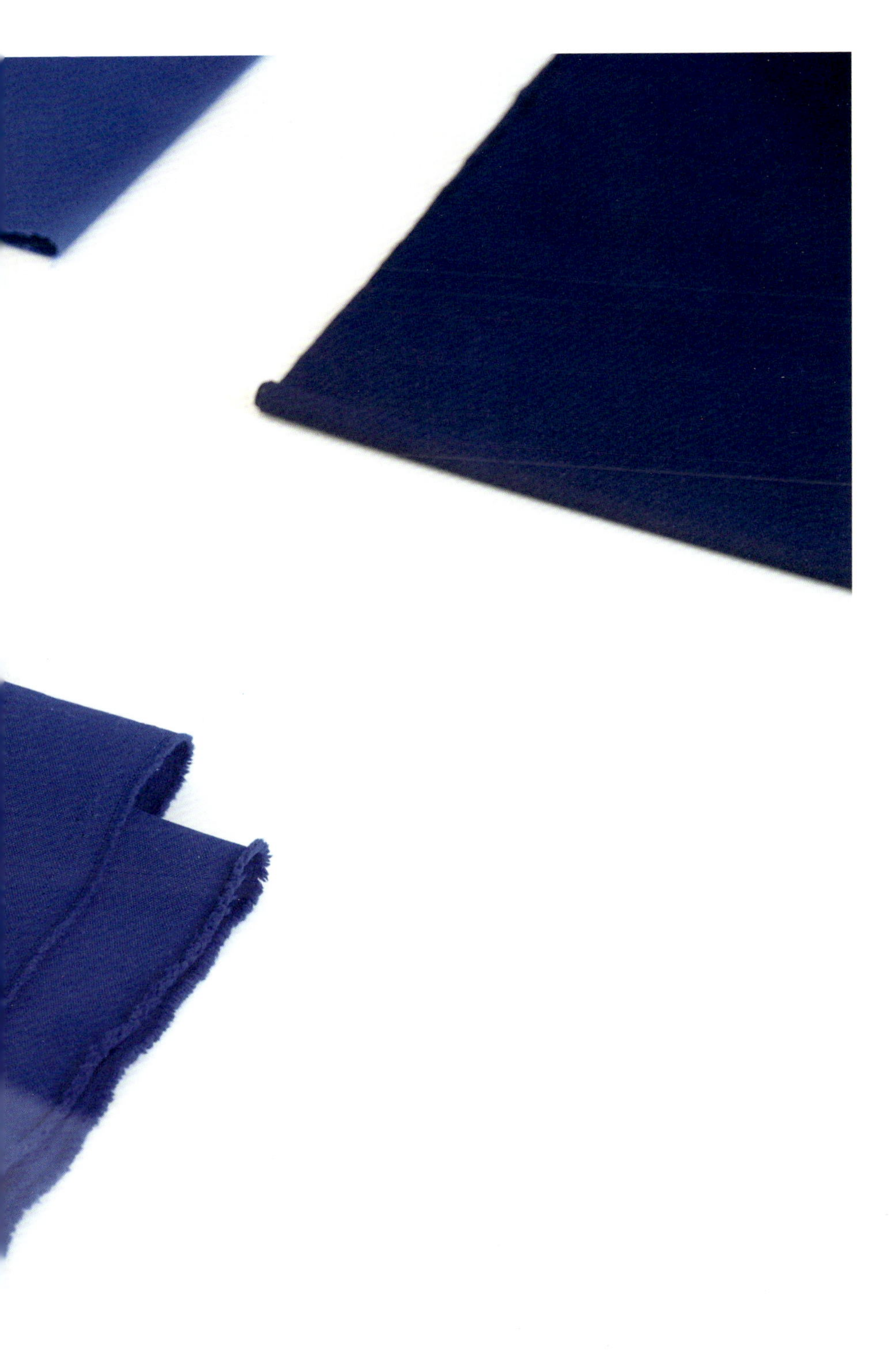

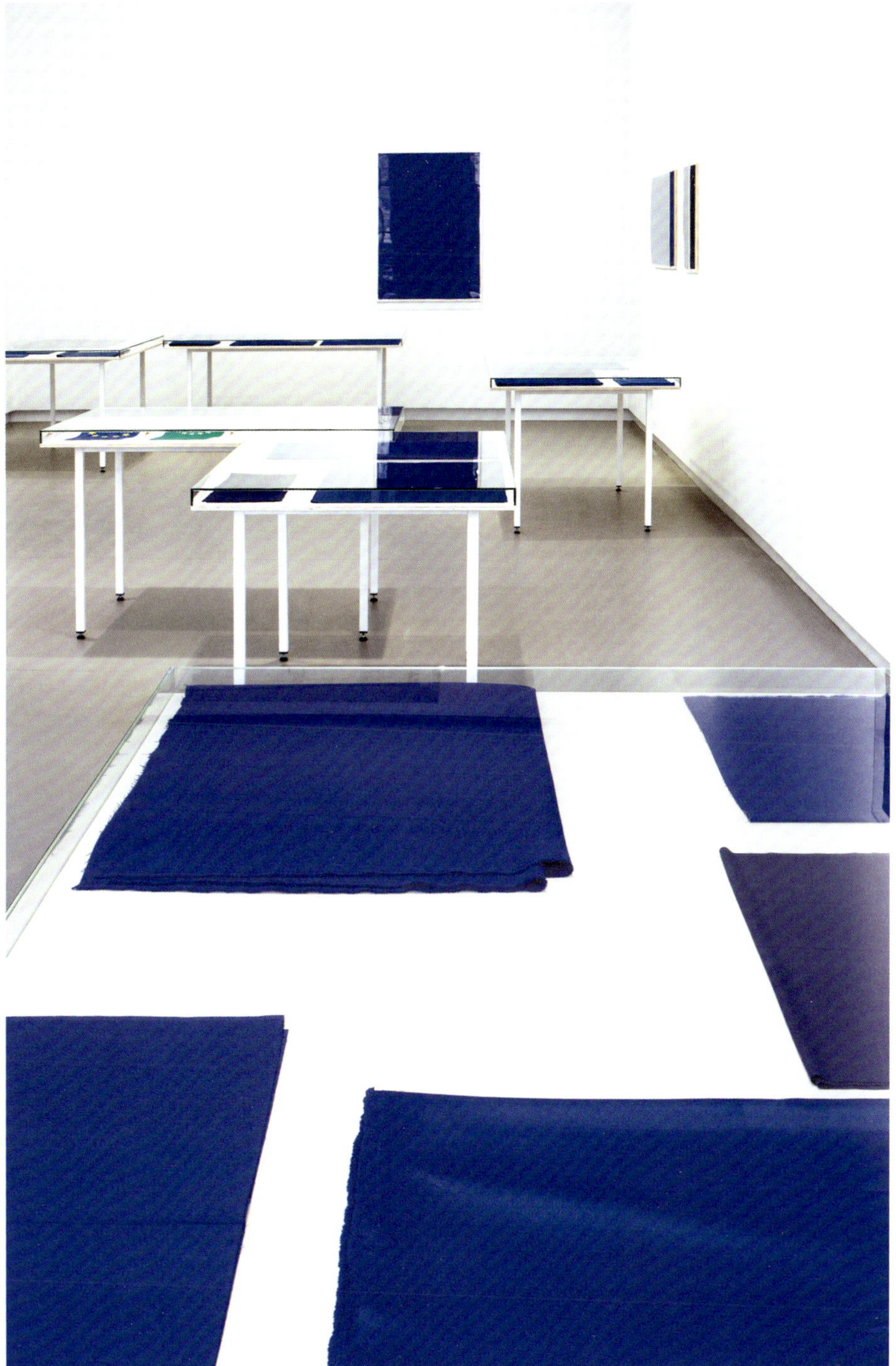

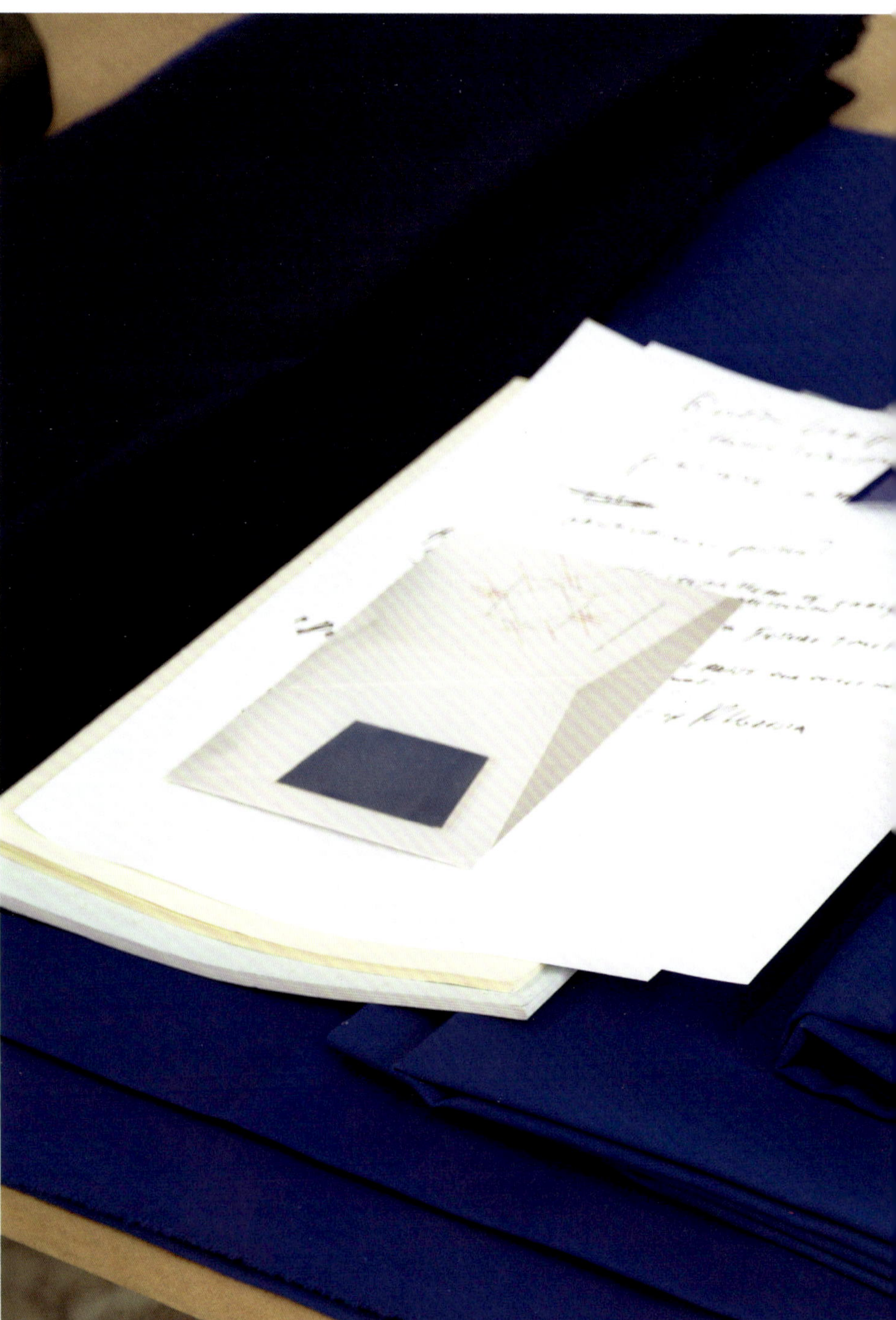

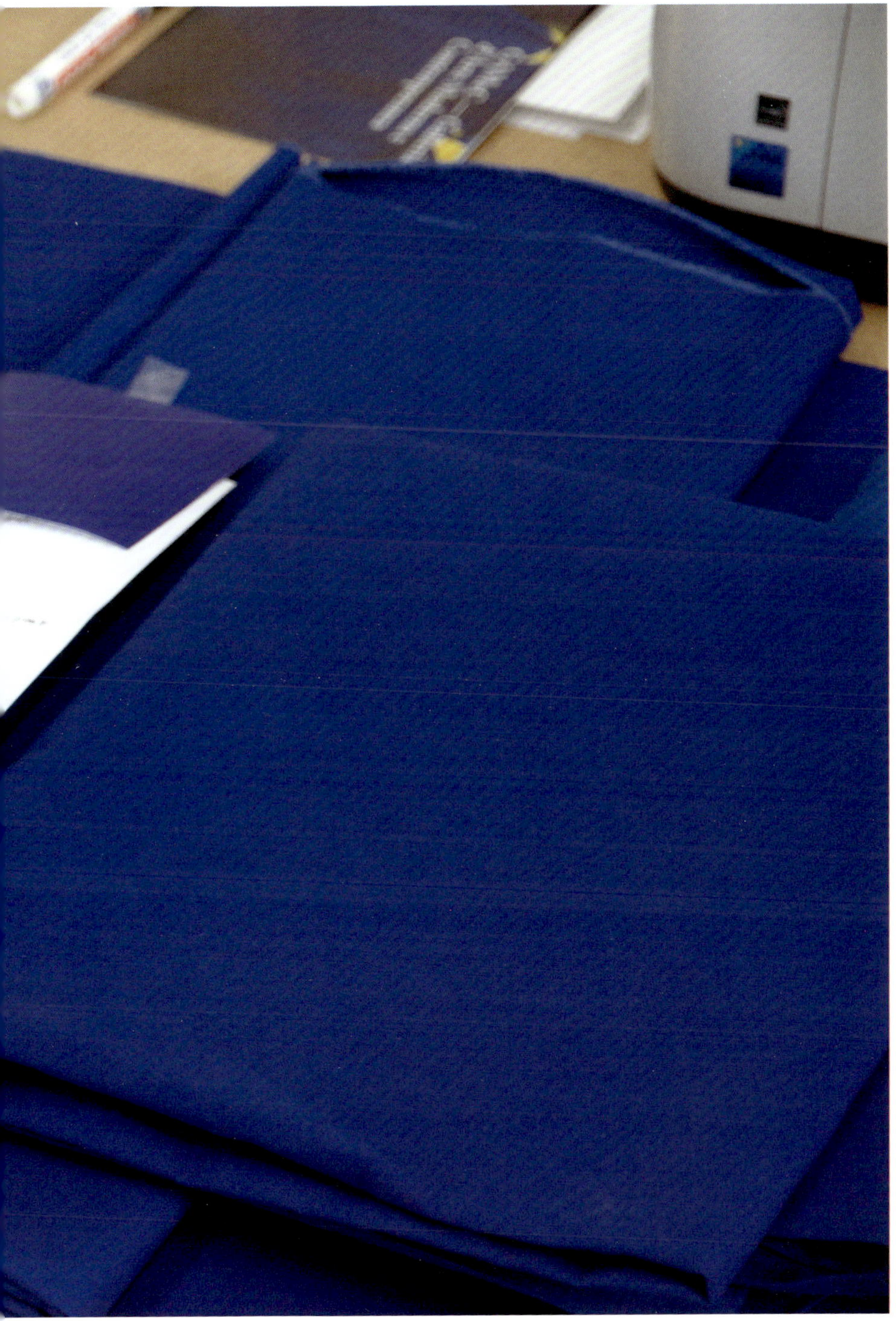

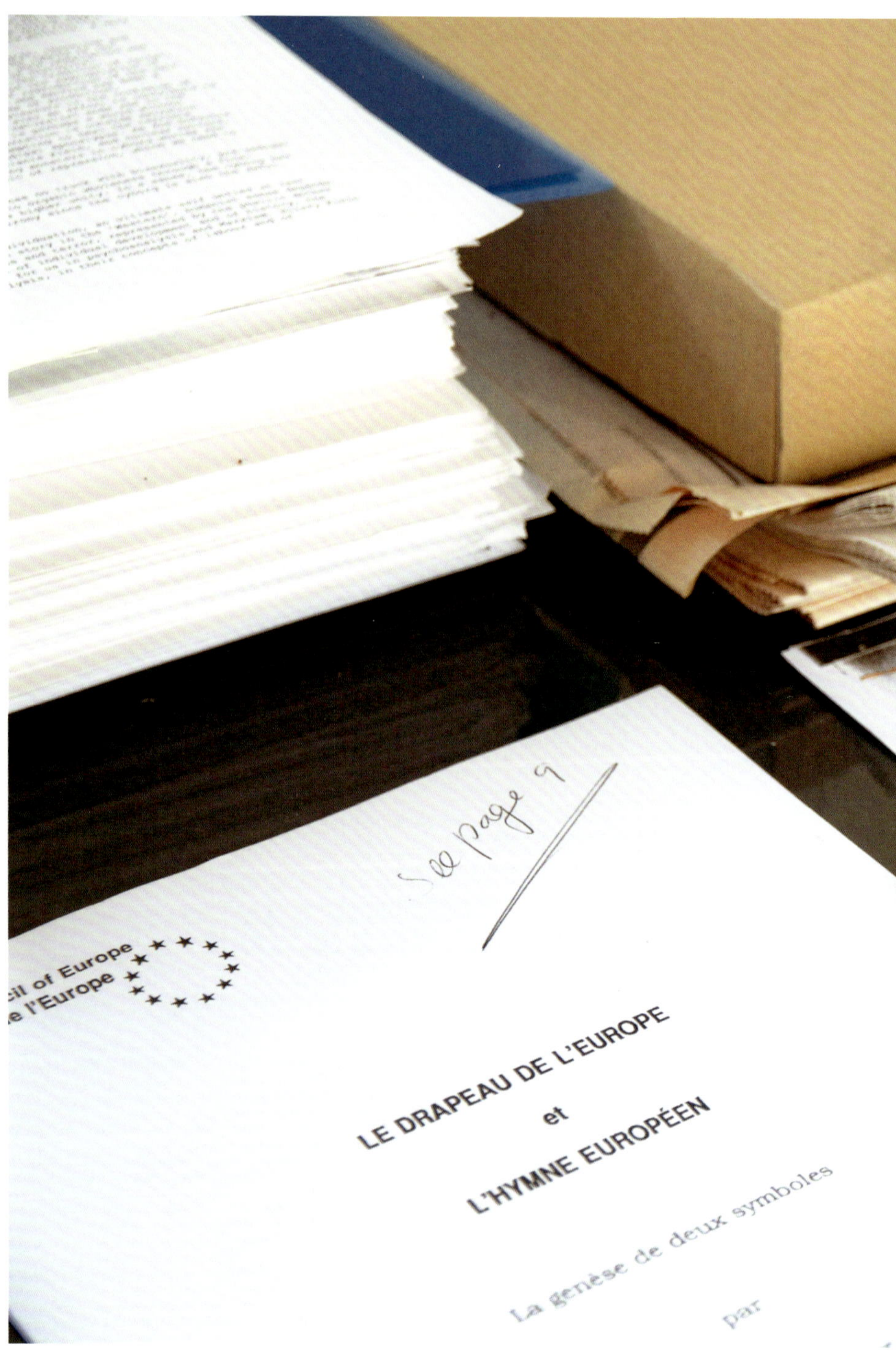
See page 9
Council of Europe
Conseil de l'Europe
LE DRAPEAU DE L'EUROPE
et
L'HYMNE EUROPÉEN
La genèse de deux symboles
par

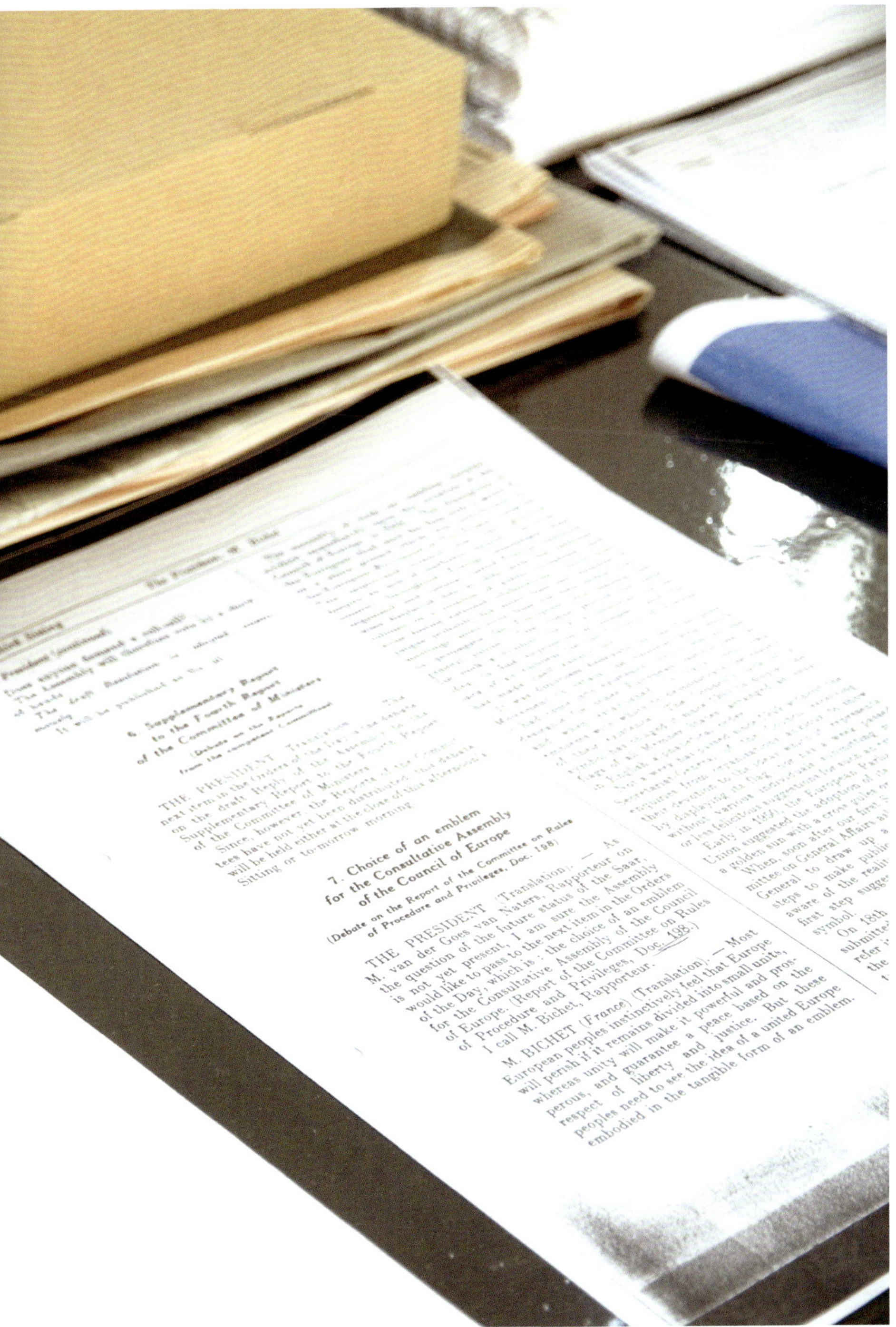

7. Choice of an emblem for the Consultative Assembly of the Council of Europe

(Debate on the Report of the Committee on Rules of Procedure and Privileges, Doc. 198)

THE PRESIDENT (Translation). — As M. van der Goes van Naters, Rapporteur on the question of the future status of the Saar, is not yet present, I am sure the Assembly would like to pass to the next item in the Orders of the Day, which is : the choice of an emblem for the Consultative Assembly of the Council of Europe. (Report of the Committee on Rules of Procedure and Privileges, Doc. 198.)

I call M. Bichet, Rapporteur.

M. BICHET (France) (Translation). — Most European peoples instinctively feel that Europe will perish if it remains divided into small units, whereas unity will make it powerful and prosperous, and guarantee a peace based on the respect of liberty and justice. But these peoples need to see the idea of a united Europe embodied in the tangible form of an emblem.

Archive

**Selected European Flag
Designs by Arsène Heitz
1951 — 1954**

112
A blue flag with a red
and white wind-flower in
the center.
'Drapeau bleu avec en
son centre une rose des
vents rouge et blanche
à huit branches'
25 December 1954

113
A blue flag with a yellow
eight-pointed star in a
red circle (and another
one without the red
circle).
'Drapeau bleu avec
une étoile jaune à huit
branches dans un
disque rouge'
12 November 1954

114
A green flag with a red
cross and a white flag
with a red cross.
'Drapeau vert à croix
rouge'
Unknown

115
Etendard given by Pope
Leo III (Charlemagne)
'Etendard remis par le
pape Léon III à
Charlemagne'
1 January 1952

116
A blue flag with nation
flag in the upper left
corner and a circle of
stars in th middle.
'Drapeau bleu avec
en haut à gauche le
drapeau turque et
italiennes entouré
d'étoile'
29 March 1953

117
A blue flag with nation
flag in the upper left
corner with circles of
stars.
'Drapeau bleu avec les
couleurs anglaises en
haut à gauche et au
centre 15 étoiles dispo-
sées en deux cercles
concentriques'
15 November 1952

118
A blue flag with nation
flag in the upper left
corner and a circle of
stars in the middle.
'Drapeau bleu avec
en haut à gauche le
drapeau france entouré
d'étoile'
29 March 1953

119
A blue flag with a star in
the centre and a circle
of stars.
'Drapeau bleu avec en
son centre une étoile
entourée de douze
étoiles secondaires'
11 September 1955

121
A blue flag with a star in
the centre and a circle
of stars.
'Drapeau bleu avec en
son centre une étoile
entourée de douze
étoiles secondaires'
Unknown

122
A blue flag with a star in
the centre and a circle
of stars.
'Drapeau bleu avec en
son centre une étoile
entourée de douze
étoiles secondaires'
Unknown

123
A blue flag with a star in
the centre and a circle
of stars.
'Drapeau bleu avec en
son centre une étoile
entourée de douze
étoiles secondaires'
Unknown

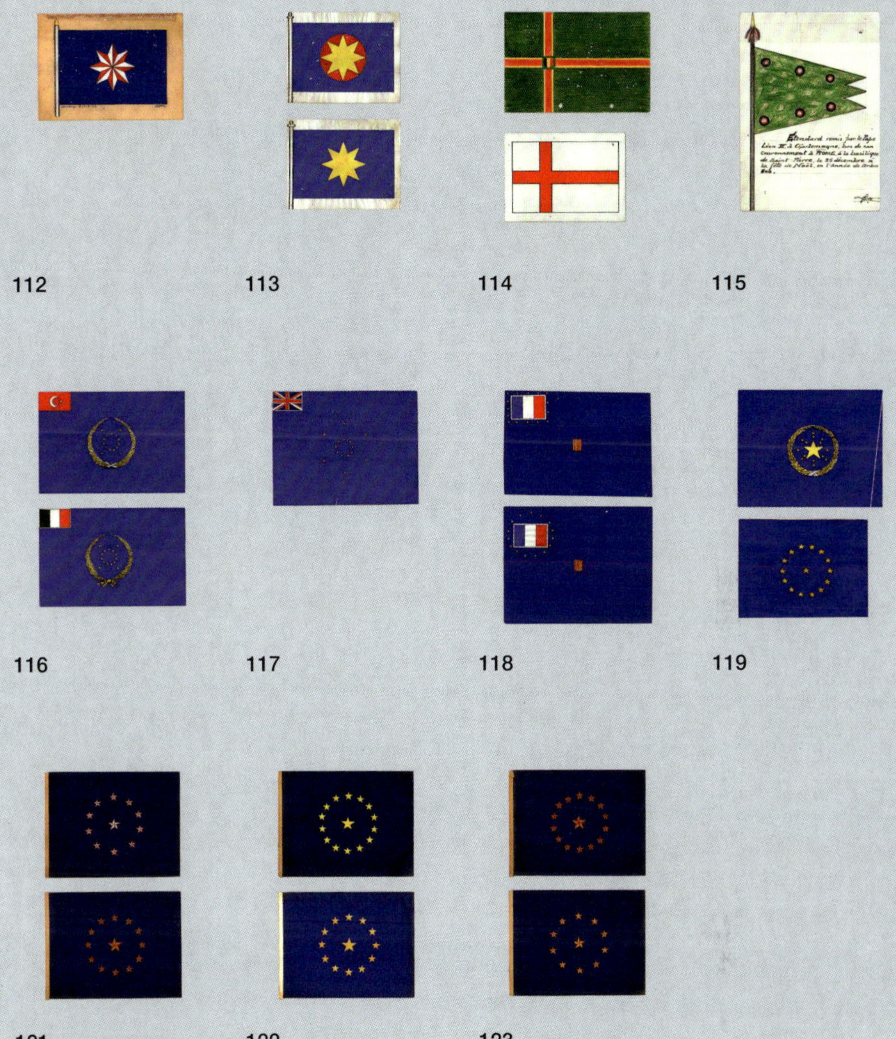

112

113

114

115

116

117

118

119

121

122

123

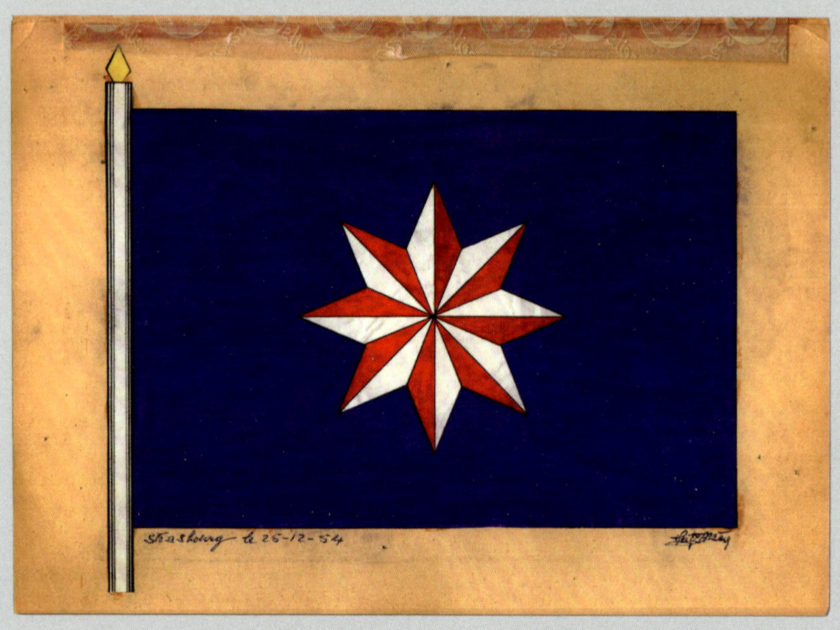

Strasbourg - le 25-12-54

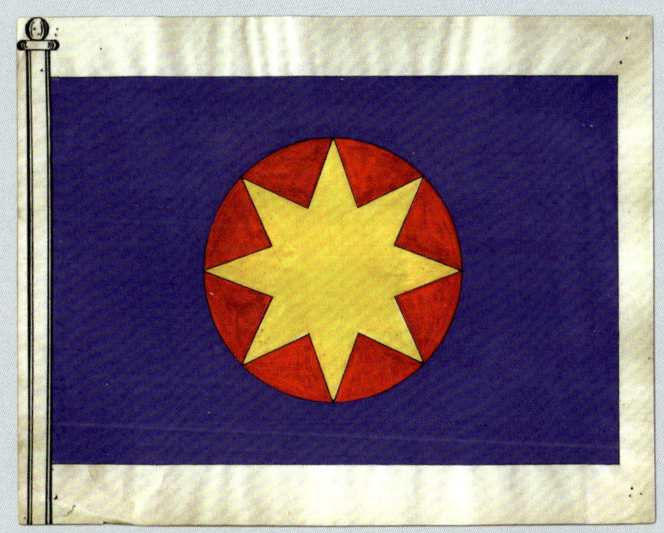

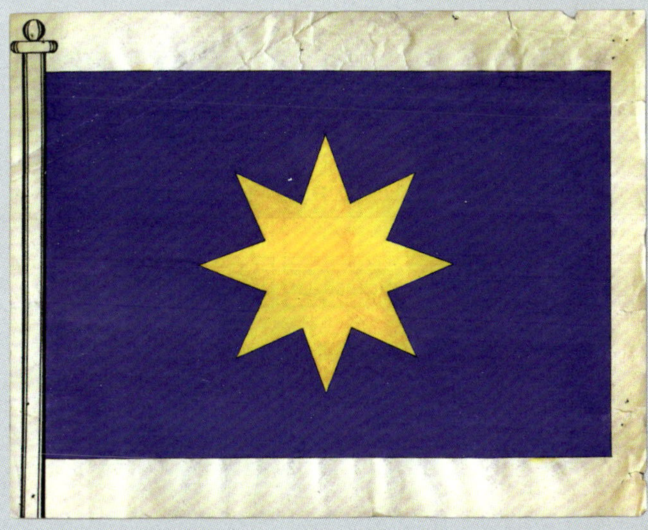

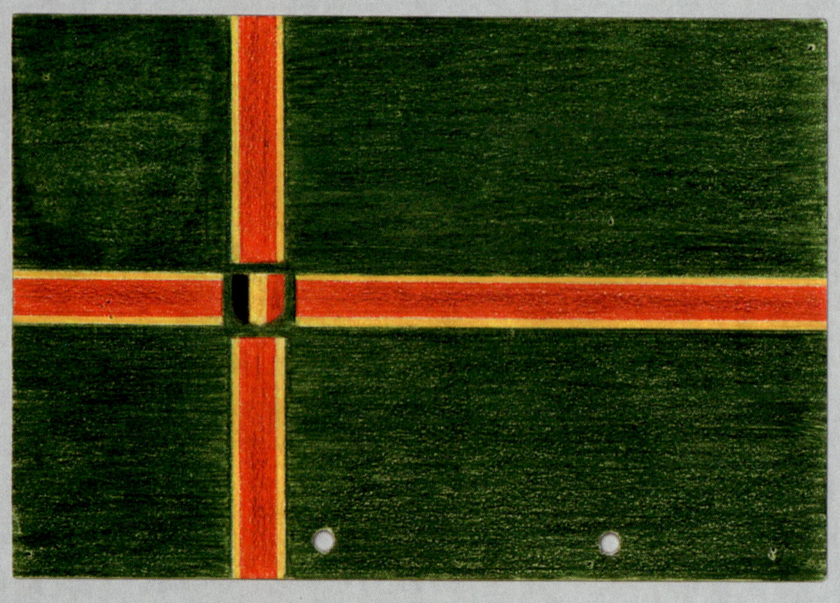

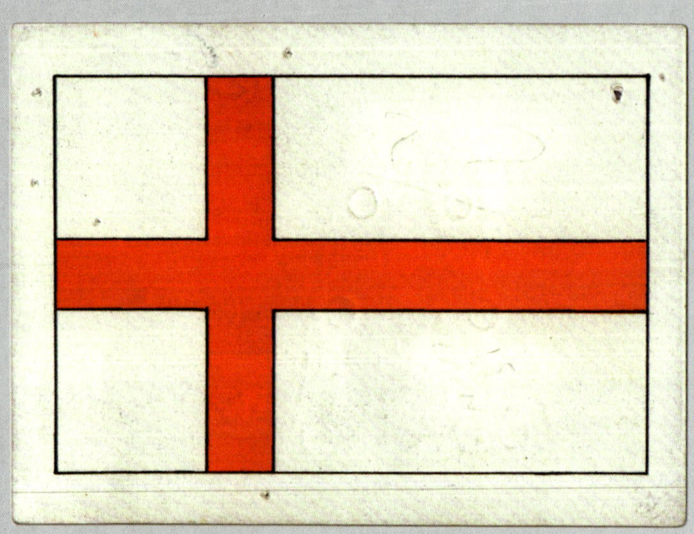

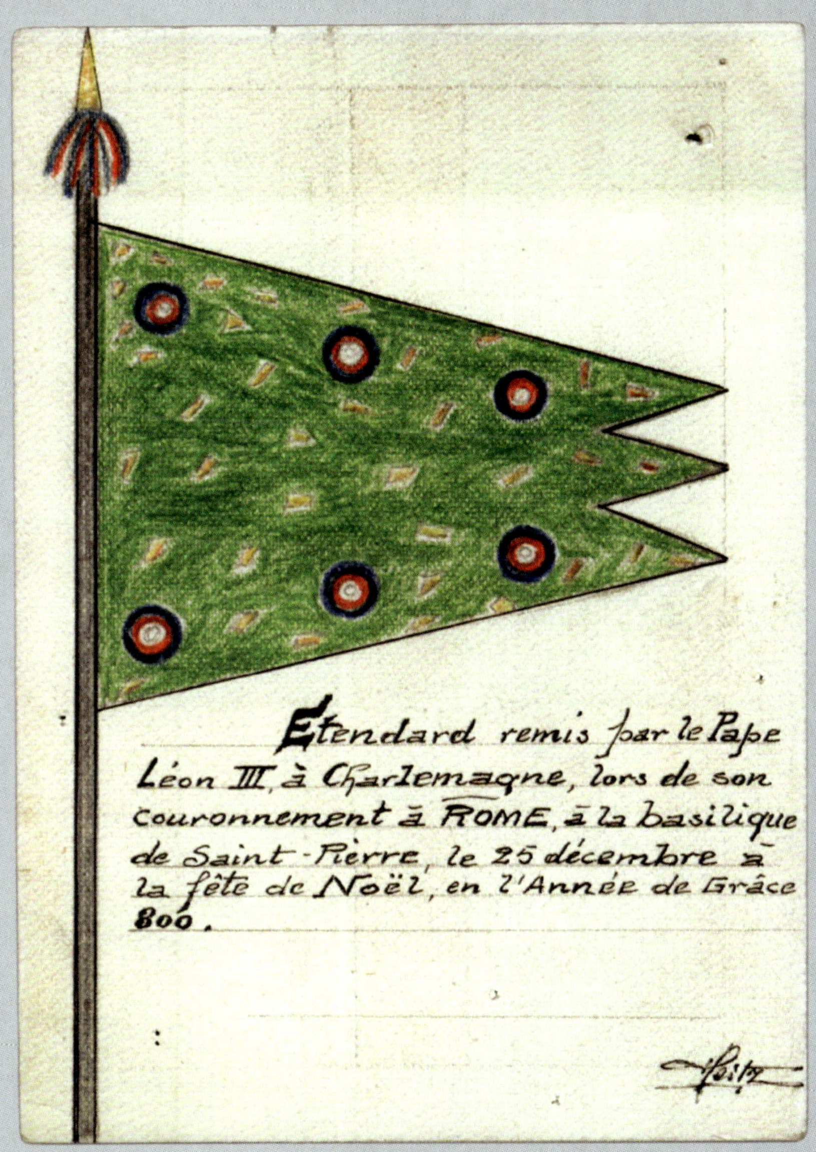

Étendard remis par le Pape Léon III, à Charlemagne, lors de son couronnement à ROME, à la basilique de Saint-Pierre, le 25 décembre à la fête de Noël, en l'Année de Grâce 800.

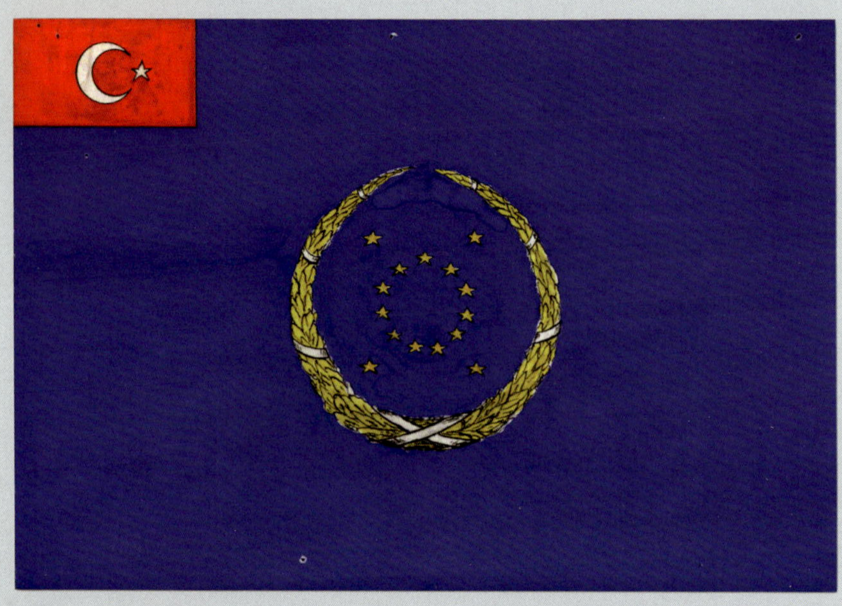

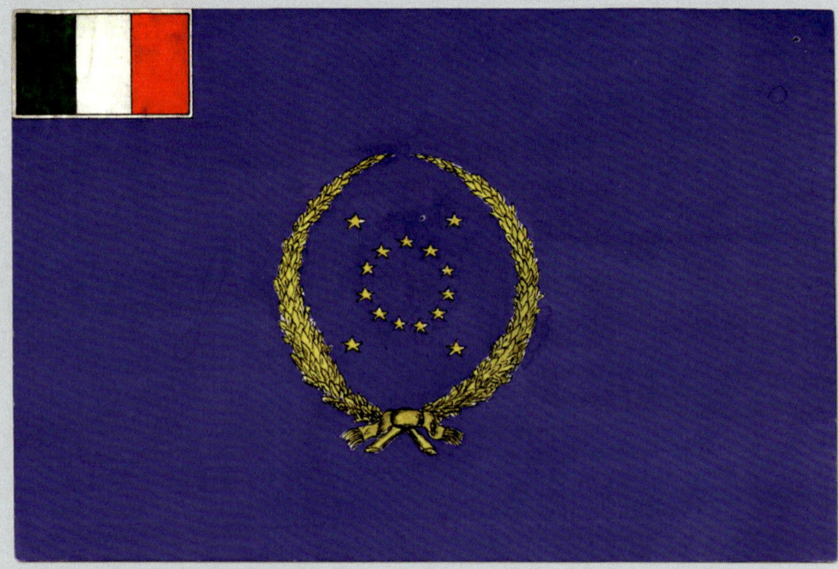

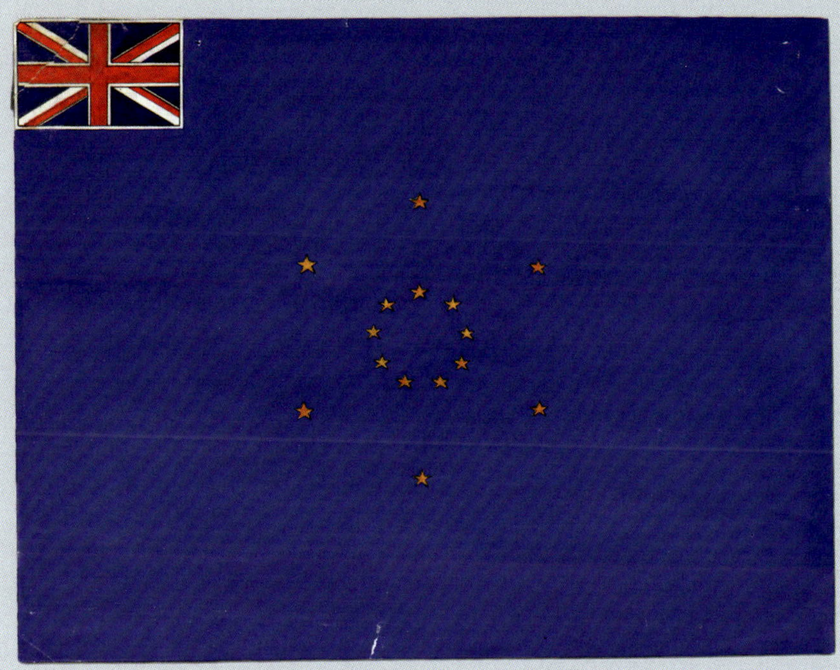

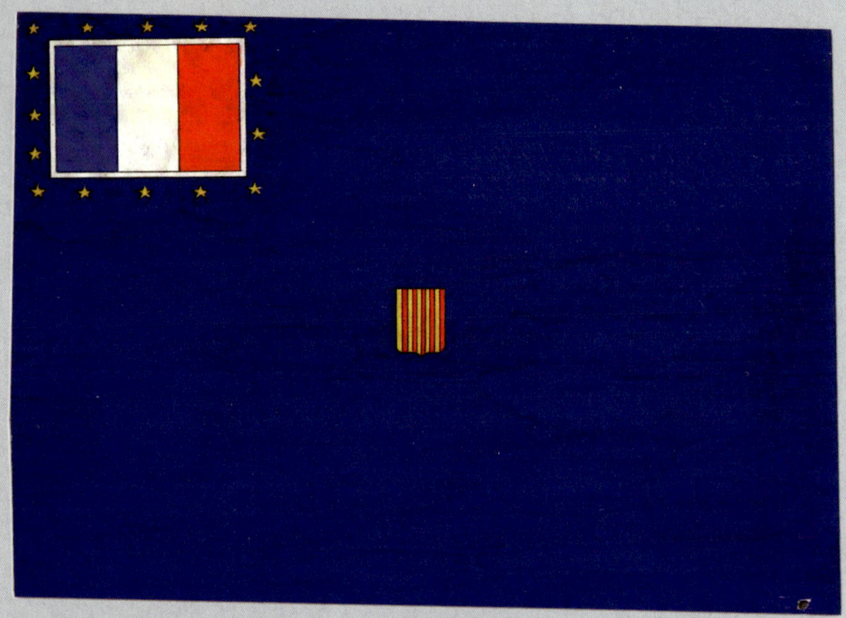

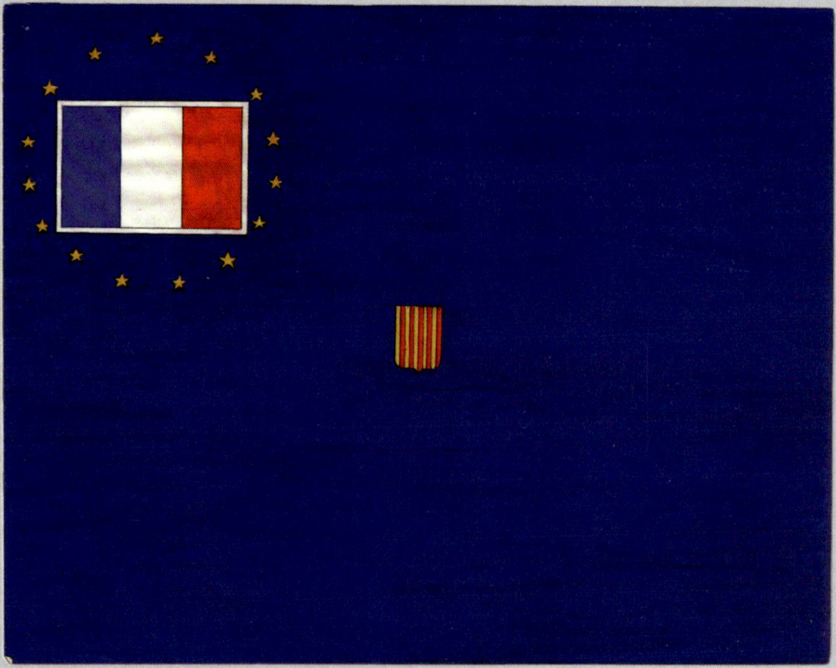

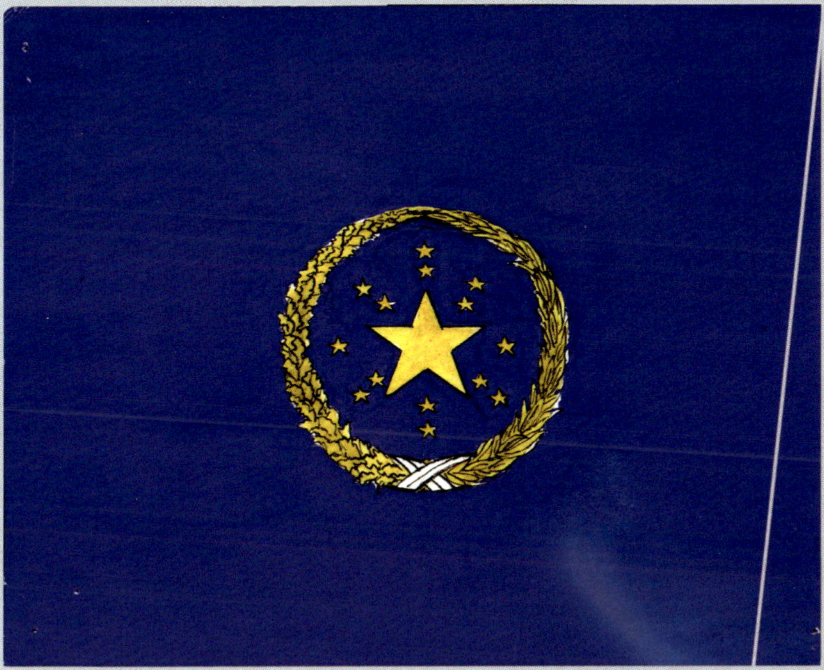

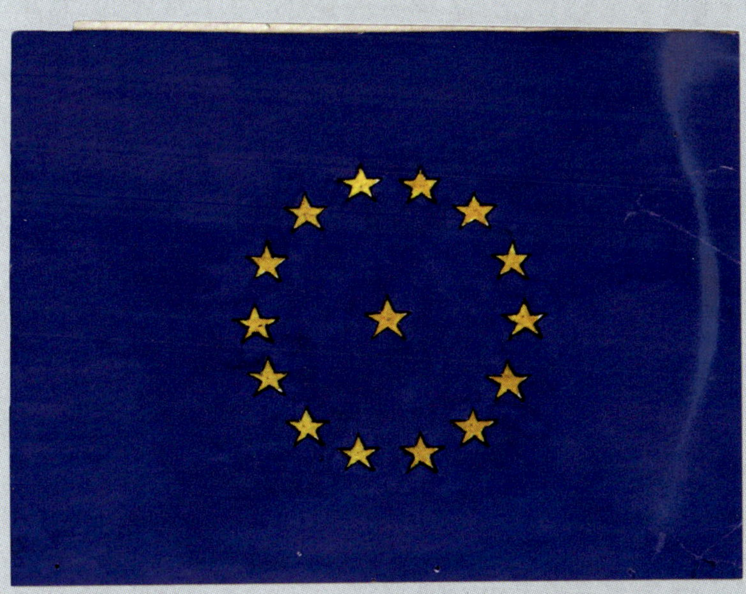

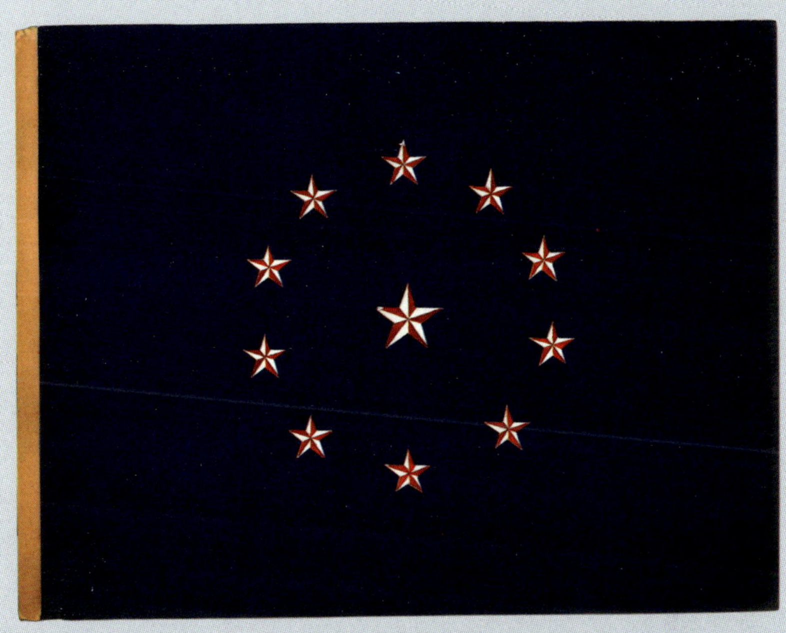

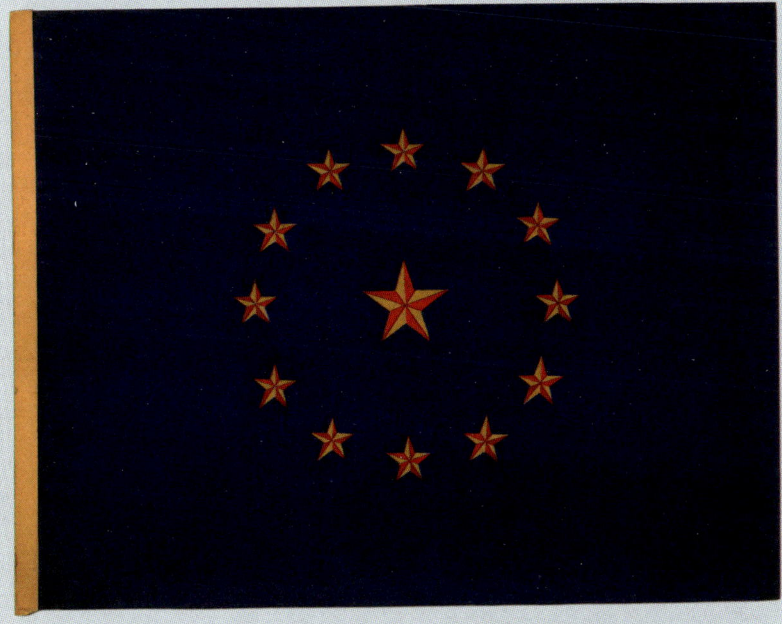

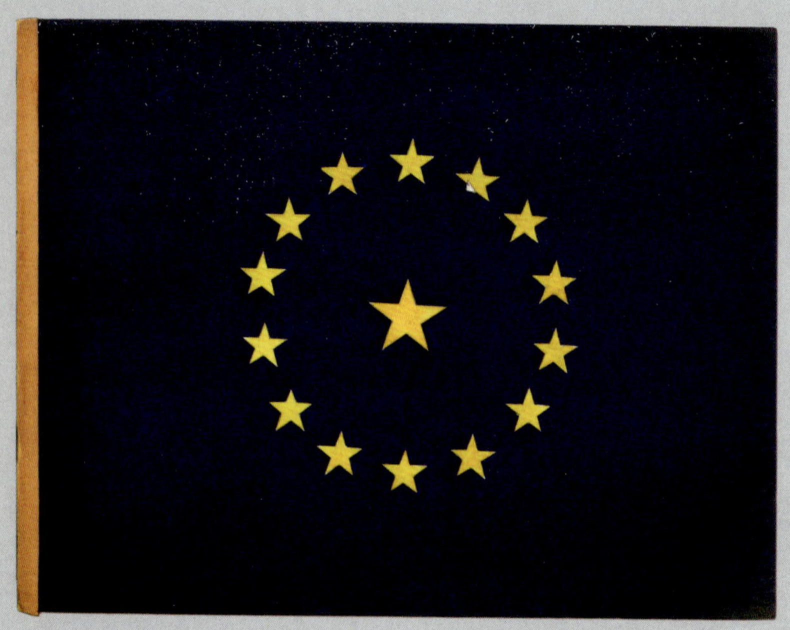

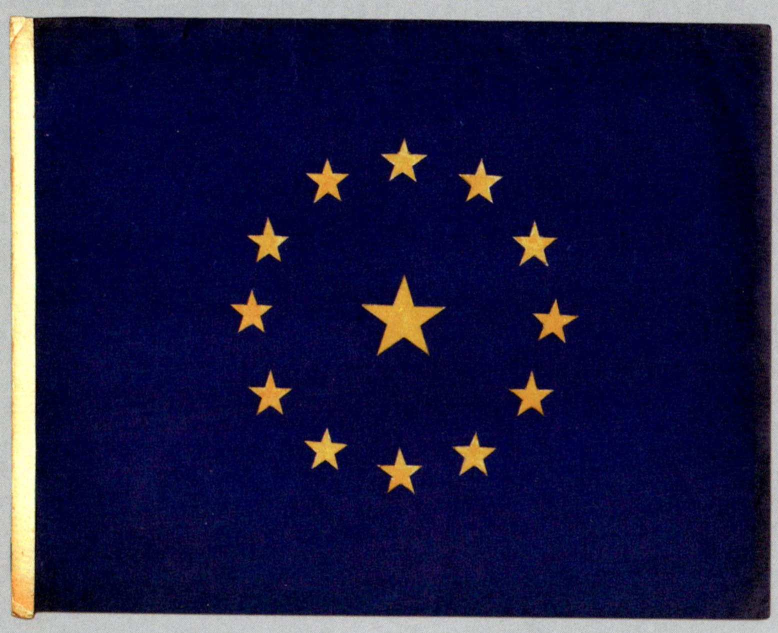

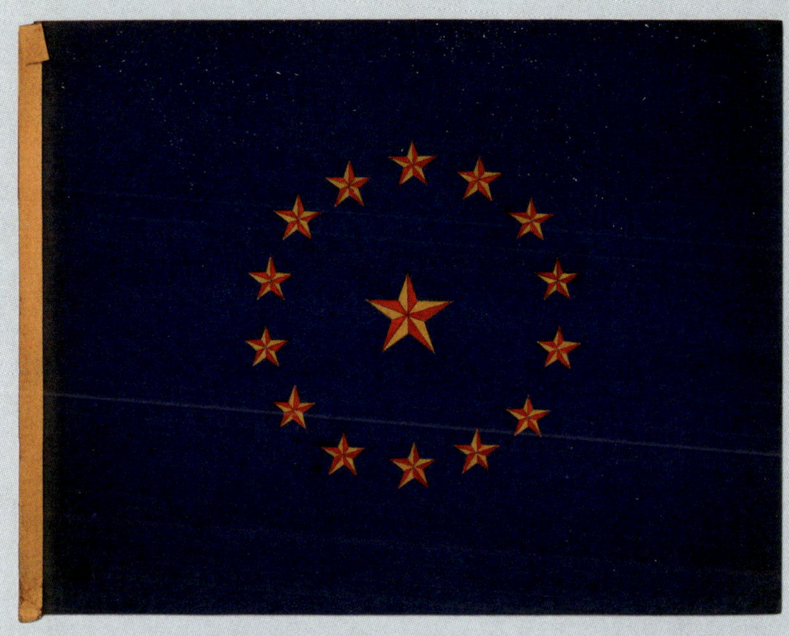

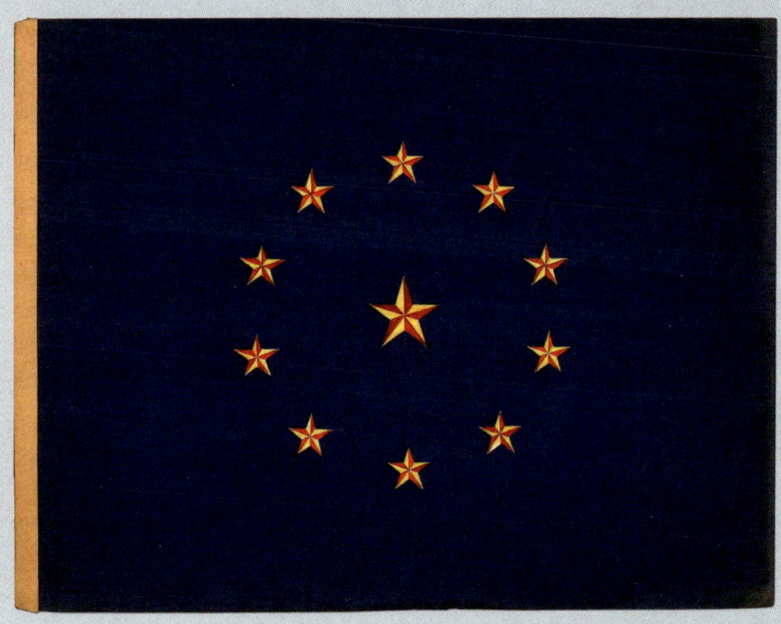

**Publications
1950 — 1955**

126
Arsène Heitz, Paul M.
G. Lévy, Paul Martin: Un
Drapeau pour l'Europe
– In Saisons d'Alsace,
no.3
12 December 1950

128
Richard Koudenhove-
Kalergi (European
Parliamentary Union)
proposes to Secretary
General that the Council
of Europe adopt the
emblem (Red Cross) of
the European
Movement
27 July 1950

132
Secretariat memo-
randum summarising 12
shortlisted proposals
Arsène Heitz to Paul M.
G. Lévy, indicating their
provenance
16 July 1951

140
Secretariat memo-
randum summarising
proposals numbered 1
to 12
15 October 1951

144
Letter from Salvador de
Madariaga to Paul M.
G. Lévy proposing blue
flag with gold stars
25 January 1952

146
The 12 proposals are
transmitted to the
Assembly
3 December 1951

150
Assembly adopts 15
point star as its own
emblem and recom-
mends that the Com-
mittee of Ministers
adopt the same as an
emblem for the Council
of Europe as a whole.
German Representa-
tive raises the issue of
the status of the Sarre
region. At the request of
Mr Kiesinger, the word
"nations" was replaced
by "members" in the
emblem description
25 September 1953

156
Assembly adopts 15
point star as its own
emblem and recom-
mends that the Com-
mittee of Ministers
adopt the same as an
emblem for the Council
of Europe as a whole.
German Representa-
tive raises the issue of
the status of the Sarre
region. At the request of
Mr Kiesinger, the word
"nations" was replaced
by "members" in the
emblem description
25 September 1953

157
Assembly adopts 15
point star as its own
emblem and recom-
mends that the Com-
mittee of Ministers
adopt the same as an
emblem for the Council
of Europe as a whole.
German Representative
raises the issue of the
status of the Sarre
region. At the request of

Mr Kiesinger, the word
"nations" was replaced
by "members" in the
emblem description
25 September 1953

158
Hallstein (Secretary of
State for Foreign Affairs
of Germany) to Secre-
tary General, pointing
out that only the Com-
mittee of Ministers has
the power to adopt
a Council of Europe
emblem
10 December 1953

160
Secretariat Memoran-
dum on the choice of an
emblem for the Council
of Europe. Makes
distinction between flag
and emblem
19 March 1954

170
Deputies adopt the 12-
star flag and accom-
panying heraldic
description
9 December 1955

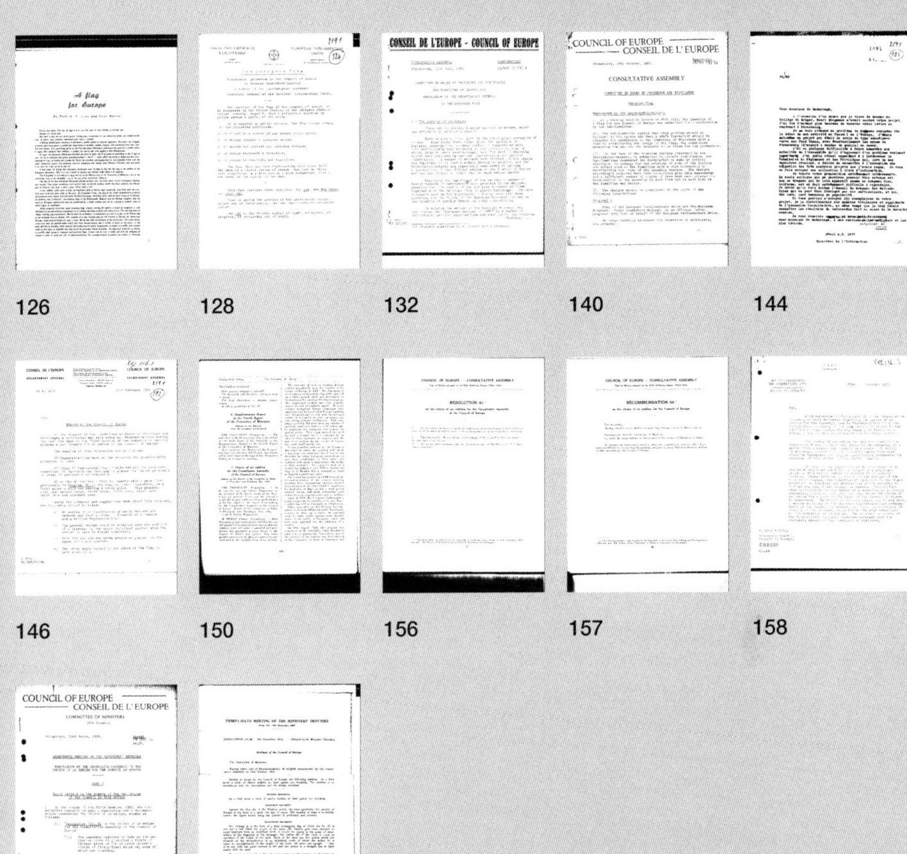

126 128 132 140 144

146 150 156 157 158

160 170

A flag for Europe

By Paul M. G. Levy and Paul Martin

Strong men smile. The day of flags is over and the coat of arms belongs to another age.
Enough for strong men.

But there is also the rest of the world. Strong men, fortunately for our distracted globe, are comparatively few. At heart, man, sensitive, emotional man, loves a symbol.

If Europe should unite tomorrow, it will need a visible symbol to rally its supporters. Moreover, the struggles of recent years have given a considerable importance to symbols ; parties, nations, and movements have their symbols and colours. The controlling spirits of the Pan-European Movement understood the need for a symbol when, in 1923, they designed their emblem : a golden sun and a red cross against a blue blackground.

In 1947, the European Movement invented the green E flag : the E of peace corresponding to the V sign of war. For let us remember that great preceding symbol — the V — under which the battle of democracy was won ; invented in 1941 in bombarded London by Victor de Laveleye and popularised by that splendid orator over the radio. Resistance papers and statesmen were its champions and among them Winston Churchill who had much to do with the origin of the E sign too.

It was under the E flag that European institutions saw the light of day but this flag is the emblem of the European Movement. Now it is the Council of Europe and Europe itself which is in question.

The E flag flew in Strasbourg in 1949 but not at the Mairie, seat of the Committee of Ministers ; not at the University, seat of the Assembly ; not at the seat of the Secretariat General.

The flag of the Pan-European Movement floated proudly over the hotel where Count Coudenhove Kalergi was staying. These great movements have perfect right to use the symbols which they have adopted, but Europe and its Council still have to find a flag. What shall it be?

A new emblem called upon to play an important part in history must necessarily have links with the past. One may recall here great flags of the past : the Crusaders Cross ; the flag of the Swiss Confederation of which the same form with colours inverted makes the Red Cross flag ; the Union Jack, with the three crosses of St-George, St-Andrew, and St-Patrick ; the tricolour flags of the Netherlands, Belgium and the Weimar Republic. But the union of European democracies must be symbolised by a single emblem and not by a group of symbols, some of which might be challenged.

Many proposals have been made including flags already existing. We believe it would be dangerous to take the flag of an already existing organisation or to combine too many symbols and colours in one. The new flag must be simple, striking, new, harmonious. But let there be no illusion ; a combination as fresh or as gay as the French flag is not invented twice in history. The creation of a new rallying sign for the Council of Europe, for democratic Europe, raises many problems not easy to solve. If one sets aside the emblems of the forerunners, who must remain active and keep the symbols under which they have become known, then it is best to return to the source : to the good old rules of heraldry which demand that a flag must be easily recognizable, as simple as possible, and recognizable at first sight on unfurled silk. One factor in particular merits attention : the flag must stand out as clearly as possible when flying in company with national flags. It must also be easy to make and with the minimum of colours in order to avoid the risk of misinterpretation. For example instead of placing the colours of National

7

flags side by side, why not use white which is in all of them and is superior to all of them? White stands for clarity, directness, modesty, joy, peace. It is the old symbol of command to which all rally. If white is accepted then what symbol should be inscribed against the white silken field of the flag? The cross would appear to be especially indicated as much for its sobriety of form as for the ideas it evokes. Let us recall that the cross has long been a privileged emblem on flags. Its arms recall the four points of the compass, and embrace the European highways meeting at Strasbourg, the cross-roads of the new Europe. Among European states nine possess the cross as a distinctive feature of their flags. Seven of these are members of the Council of Europe. The United Kingdom, Norway, Sweden, Denmark, Iceland, the Saar, Greece. The others are Finland and Switzerland.

The crosses on these flags are blue, white, red, yellow. White may be set aside as the colour of the new cross as it is the colour of the field of the new flag. Red and blue are the most frequent colours. They should not, therefore, figure in the new flag. Yellow, the colour of the Swedish cross, cannot be used in any case against a white background for it would give a blurred effect, metal on metal, gold on silver, and unrecognizable at a certain distance. There remains green. Green has many advantages. Symbolical, it expresses rebirth, eagerness, youth, vitality, vivacity and lastly hope — that immense hope with which the European people face their future. Green has another advantage; white and green are the colours of the European Movement. It would be right to render homage to the pioneers in this way. In the same context a cross would also constitute a tribute to the creators of the Pan-European Movement.

Finally, and in order to perpetuate the part of the town of Strasbourg as seat of the Council of Europe, the shield argent with bend Gules of the old city should be inscribed on the centre of the cross where the arms intersect at the cross-roads of Europe.

The composition of the new emblem might then be defined as follows : white silk with a green cross charged at the centre with the arms of the town of Strasbourg which, translated into heraldic terms is « a cross vert on a field argent, at the centre a shield argent with bend Gules ».

The new flag would correspond with the requirements which we have emphasized above : clarity, simplicity, easily recognizable and easy to make.

May this piece of silk, with its folds floating proudly before the massed flags of the European nations, affirm by its presence the force of an ideal : Peace and the union of the peoples.

8

The European Flag

Memorandum presented to the Council of Europe
by Richard Coudenhove-Kalergi
President of the Pan-European Mouvement
Secretary General of the European Parliamentary Union.

The question of the flag of the Council of Europe, to
be discussed by the Second Session of the European Consultation Assembly, ought to find a definitive solution by
giving Europe a symbol of its unity.

To be adopted by public opinion, the flag should comply
to the following conditions:

1) It should be a symbol of our common civilisation;

2) It should present a European emblem;

3) It should not provoke any national rivalry;

4) It should represent a tradition,

5) It should be beautiful and dignified.

The flag that has been representing ever since 1923,
the idea of a United States of Europe, complies to these
five conditions: a golden sun on a blue background, with a
red cross in the middle of the sun.

*

This flag combines three symboles: the Sun, the Red Cross,
the Blue Sky.

Thus it unites the symbols of the greco-latin civilisation and of Christianity, the two basic elements of modern
Europe.

The Sun is the eternal symbol of light, of spirit, of
progress, of prosperity and of truth.

The Red Cross is being recogniced by the while world, by christian and non-christian nations, as a symbol of international charity and of the brotherhood of man.

The Cross has been, since the fall of the Roman Empire, the great symbol of Europe's moral unity. It is but natural that this symbol should figure within the European Flag - just as it appears on the flags of Switzerland, of Great Britain, Sweden, Norway, Danmark and other european nations.

The crushing majority of European christians will not admit the cross being removed from the European flag - while the none-christian minority cannot oppose this symbol, inseparable from our history and civilisation; as the christian minorities in the Near East do not oppose the national symboles of the Crescant and the Star of David.

The Blue Sky, the natural background of the Sun, is a symbol of peace. Blue is bound to be the basic color of the European flag, since all other colors have at present a special meaning: the red flag = bolshevism; the green flag = islam; the yellow flag = quarantains; the black flag = mourning; the white flag = capitulation.

The Emblem.

Europe should have an Emblem, connected with its flag, to serve as an instrument of propaganda - as the Soviet-Star serves bolshevism and the Svastica served hitlerism.

Such a European Emblem constitutes the center of the flag of the U.S.E.: the red-cross on the golden (yellow) sun. Without colors, it is a cross in a circle.

This design has been found, as a pre-christian symbol of world-harmony, on celtic and germanic monuments.

National neutrality.

The flag of the U.S.E. has no national character, since it has no resemblance with any national flag. Thus it avoids the dangers of misinterpretations that would arise if letters of the alphabeth were used as elements of the European Flag. The letter E, for instance, meaning "Europe", might also be read for "England", the letter F, meaning "Federation", for"France", the letter D, meaning "Democracy", for "Deutschland", the letter U, meaning "Union", for "U.S.A." or " USSR" with all the fatal consequences of such interpretations.

Tradition.

The red cross that constitutes the center of the flag, has been undoubtedly the first European Flag at the time of the Crusades.

Combined with the sun on a blue background, it has become the most ancient symbol of the european idea. Since 1923 this flag has been adapted throughout Europe, as symbol of the Pan-European Movement. Acclaimed by the first Pan-European Congress in Vienna in 1926, this flag has floated over the roofs of Geneva, to great in 1929 the European Initiative of Aristide Briand, the Honorary Chairman of the Pan-European Union.

After the war, the European Parliamentary Union, that has launched the idea of a European Parliament elected by the national parliaments, has adopted this flag in December 1947, by an unanimous vote of its Council.

<u>Beauty and Dignity.</u>

The evident beauty and dignity of this flag have never been contested.

**

All these reasons recommend the adoption of this flag by the Council of Europe.

Should the Council choose another symbol of its present structure of an association of sovereign nations, our flag will, under all circumstances, continue to be the symbol of the struggle for a European Federation - up to the birthday of the Unites States of Europe.

Gstaad, 27 July 1950.

R. Coudenhove-Kalergi.

CONSEIL DE L'EUROPE - COUNCIL OF EUROPE

COMMITTEE ON RULES OF PROCEDURE AND PRIVILEGES

Sub-Committee on Immunities

MEMORANDUM OF THE SECRETARIAT GENERAL

ON THE EUROPEAN FLAG

1.- The purpose of an Emblem

There are no ideals, however exalted in nature, which can afford to do without a symbol.

Symbols play a vital part in the ideological struggles of to-day. Ever since there first arose the question of European organisation, a large number of suggestions have more particularly been produced in its connection, some of which, despite their shortcomings, have for want of anything better been employed by various organisations and private individuals. A number of writers have pointed out how urgent and important it is that a symbol should be adopted, and the Secretariat-General has repeatedly been asked to provide a description of the official emblem of the Council of Europe and has been forced to admit that no such emblem exists.

Realising the importance of the matter, a number of French Members of Parliament[1] have proposed in the National Assembly that the symbol of the European Movement be flown together with the national flag on public buildings. Private movements such as the Volunteers of Europe have also been agitating for the flying of the European Movement colours on the occasion of certain French national celebrations.

In Belgium the emblem of the European Movement was used during the "European Seminar of 1950" by a number of individuals, private organisations and even public institutions

/Certain......

A 5445
Tf 260/VT

---

(1) Proposal submitted by M. Bichet and colleagues.

Certain newspapers criticised the use of this emblem and expressed their regret that the Council of Europe had adopted it........which is untrue.

At Strasbourg the "E" flag has been widely used during Sessions, but to the surprise of the public, although it has been hoisted on private houses it has never been flown from French official buildings or buildings of the Council of Europe.   On the other hand, a considerable amount of rivalry has manifested itself at the Seat of the Council inasmuch as the blue flag with the golden sun and red cross of the European Parliamentary Union has also made an appearance there.

This latter emblem, created by Count Coudenhove-Kalergi in 1923, is still used by him.   The green "E" emblem dates from the early days of the European Movement.   Both, however, are private emblems which do not affect the problem of a Council of Europe flag and its official use.

In August 1950, the Assembly examined the Report drawn up by the Secretariat-General at the request of the Committee on General Affairs on practical measures designed to make the peoples of Europe more directly aware of their unity. The Assembly referred the various chapters of this Report to the Committees qualified to deal with them.   One of the measures advocated was the adoption of a flag.   This proposal is a matter for the Committee on Rules of Procedure and Privileges to decide (AS/AG (50) 85).

2.- <u>Design of the emblem of the Council of Europe and its use</u>

The Assembly must reach a decision as to the principle of adopting an emblem, as to its design and the use to which it is to be put.   This last point will briefly be dealt with here, partly on the basis of procedure and regulations established by the United Nations in a similar connection.

The text to be submitted to the Assembly for later recommendation to the Committee of Ministers might read as follows:

"The Consultative Assembly recommends to the Committee of Ministers:

<u>Article 1</u>: That the emblem of the Council of Europe shall be..... .... (description).

<u>Article 2</u>: That the Governments of Member States shall use the emblem of the Council of Europe conjointly with the national flag on all official buildings and on all occasions when flags are officially required to be flown, including the 5th May of each year, the anniversary date of the signing

/of the ......

of the Statute of the Council of Europe.

In cases where it is flown together with a national flag, that of the Council of Europe shall be placed to the right of the national flag.

Article 3: The emblem of the Council of Europe shall be flown:

(a) On all buildings of the Council of Europe;

(b) On the official residence of the Secretary-General and Deputy Secretaries-General;

(c) On all vehicles used by the Chairman of the Committee of Ministers, the President and Vice-Presidents of the Consultative Assembly, the Secretary-General and the Deputy Secretaries-General, whenever these personages are riding in the vehicles.

Article 4: The specialised authorities established within the Council of Europe and the non-governmental organisations recognised by the latter shall be entitled to use the Council flag subject to conditions to be laid down by order of the Secretary-General.

Article 5: The flag of the Council of Europe may be used by individuals of the Member States provided it is at all times treated with respect.

Article 6: The Secretary-General shall be responsible for the carrying out of these provisions."

3.- Design of the Emblem

It would seem wiser not to adopt any flag already existing. Some are already employed by certain organisations, which should continue to use them. A completely new flag must be designed; on the other hand, any proposals submitted to this effect should fulfil the following requirements:

(a) Sufficient symbolical significance;

(b) Simplicity;

(c) Legibility;

(d) Harmony

(e) Pleasing appearance;

(f) Orthodox heraldic design.

/A. Symbols......

A. Symbols proposed

A very large number of symbols have been suggested.
Those most frequently mentioned may be classified as follows:

- A cross - symbol of Christian civilisation, of
  Europe's crossroads (North - South, East -
  West), of command; reminiscent of the
  Crusades; the only symbol common to half
  the flags of Member States (Denmark, Greece,
  Iceland, Norway, Saar, Sweden, United
  Kingdom). Sometimes, as a variant, the
  Cross of St. Andrew, symbol of the Grand
  Duke of Burgundy, which appears historically
  the most appropriate.

- An "E" - Used by the European Movement, sometimes
  improved by being detached from the border
  of the flag, but criticized by experts in
  heraldry as being "more of a signpost than
  a flag".

- A white star in a circle - used in 1944-45 by the armies
  of liberation.

- Multiple stars - equivalent to the number of Member
  States in the Council of Europe and appearing
  either in the form of green stars on a white
  ground, white stars on a red ground, or
  silver stars for the Associate Members and
  golden stars for full Members.

- The coat-of-arms of the Town of Strasbourg - Argent,
  a bend gules, symbolising the official Seat
  of the Council of Europe.

- A sun - representing dawning hope.

- A triangle - representing culture.

B. Colours proposed

Some have suggested a combination of all the colours
already used for the various flags of Europe. One of the
earliest proposals sent in by a Strasbourg citizen was even
accompanied by a statistical study of the colours employed,
and was designed in blue, green, yellow, black, white and
red in proportion to the extent these colours occur in the
national flags. Green and white, the colours of the
European Movement, are more often suggested; it should
perhaps be pointed out in this respect that the original
motive indulging the choice of green by Mr. Duncan Sandys

/was the use.....

was the use of the complementary colour to red; this has,
however, been generally overlooked and green is advocated
rather as symbolising youth and hope.   On the other hand,
some people have held that the true heraldic colour for
Europe is blue (just as black is the colour for Africa, yellow
for Asia and green for Australia); it has not been possible
to trace the origin of this theory.

     C.   While it is true that an orthodox heraldic device
and adequate symbolic significance are of some importance, good
visual recognition, attraction to the eye, and facility of
reproduction are even more essential.   When first examining
the proposals received, it therefore appeared wiser straight
away to reject:

     (a) All intricate designs bearing symbols difficult
          to draw or particularly complicated to reproduce;

     (b) Clashing colour combinations, however ingenious.

     (c) Multicoloured emblems on the diagonal - such as
          the Cross of Burgundy - too reminiscent of the house
          flags of shipping companies.

     The reasons militating against the use of emblems
of existing Movements (European Parliamentary Union and
European Movement) have already been given above.

     D.   Main proposals advanced

     All proposals have been submitted to the members of the
Committee.   It is, however, in practice impossible to describe
them all.   Below will be found those proposals which appeared
most worthy of the Committee's attention:

(a) The Manné proposal: This is the above-mentioned Strasbourg
proposal based on the statistical distribution of the various
colours on the European flags.   Its design is in the form of
four horizontal stripes - blue, green, yellow and black
(secondary colours) - a triangle in red and white, the dominant
colours, being placed adjacent to the pole.   These colours
(red and white) are not only those most frequently found on
European flags, but also constitute the colours of the Town
of Strasbourg.   Every European will find in this composite
flag the colours with which he himself is familiar.

(b) The Martin-Levy proposal: Designed by one of the curators
of the Strasbourg Museum and a member of the Secretariat-General.
White silk ground with a green cross bearing in the centre the
coat-of-arms of the Town of Strasbourg.   This flag resembles
the colours of the European Movement and thus pays tribute to
the founders of the Council of Europe; the cross, symbol of

                           /Christianity......

Christianity, is also the symbol of Europe's highways
(North, South, East and West) at the converging point of
which stands Strasbourg (the city of crossroads).   This
design is easily copied and is particularly harmonious to
the eye, especially if the cross is shifted slightly towards
the pole in the manner of Scandinavian flags.

        This design met with considerable approval, but also
with some criticism for the following reasons:

    (i)   White is easily soiled.   It is therefore better
          not to have a flag with a white ground;

    (ii) No federal flag has so far borne the coat-of-arms
          of the capital as its central motif.

    (iii) Exception can be taken to the cross.

(c)   The Coudenhove proposal: Count Coudenhove-Kalergi
favours the white flag bearing a red cross whose four branches
extend to the edges of the flag - i.e. the flag of St. George.

(d)   The Prince de Schwarzenberg proposal: The latter proposes
that the "first European symbol" - the labarum of Constantine -
be adopted; that is, a red flag with a yellow cross.

(e)   The Lucien Philippe proposal: Fifteen green stars in
three rows on a white ground.

(f)   The Wirion proposals: Monsieur Wirion, the Luxembourg
expert in heraldry, considers that green and white should
in all events be retained.   He proposes various combinations
(a star with eight forked points, the Burgundy Cross, a
white sun on a field of green, etc.) but prefers a design
based on the Martin-Levy proposal, reversing the colours
(field of green and white cross) and doing away with the
Strasbourg coat-of-arms.   M. Wirion, however, at the beginning of March 1950, said he agreed that the white ground should
be left, even though it is easily soiled.   He was willing
to accept the white ground with a green cross provided the
Strasbourg coat-of-arms at the centre was only used for the
pennants of Council personages and flags flown on Council
buildings.   In all other cases the coat-of-arms should be
omitted.

(g)   The Sommier proposal: Monsieur Sommier of Neuilly
suggests that the aesthetic shortcomings of the "E" of the
European Movement be remedied by detaching it from the edges
of the flag and creating a neat geometrical design; this
design he has studied in detail.

(h)   Mondon proposals: Monsieur Mondon, a cartographer of

/Bad Godesberg.......

Bad Godesberg, has proposed a white triangle, symbol of culture, on various fields.

(i) Muller proposal: Monsieur Muller of Wiesbaden proposes a red flag bearing the word "Europa" in gold lettering, with a golden sun and a white hand making the sign of the oath.

(j) Harmignies proposal: Suggests the creation of a new heraldic device - a Cross of Europe on similar lines to the Cross of Lorraine, Toulouse, Malta, Jerusalem, etc. The Cross of Europe would consist of four "E"s backed on to a square. This proposal was accompanied by a series of designs demonstrating its effect on coats-of-arms, flags, pennants, medals, etc.

(k) Poucher proposal: As far back as 1939, Monsieur Poucher proposed a federal banner which was virtually the reverse of the flag of the United States of America, with blue bands and a red quarter in one corner.

(l) H. C. proposal: A European flag decorated with the internationl code sign of the letter "E". This flag would be divided horizontally into two halves, the upper blue and the lower red. These two colours also correspond to those generally adopted by the right and left wing parties respectively The flag would be distinguishable from the flag of the City of Paris, which is also blue and red, by being divided horizontally.

It will be for the Committee to choose between these various proposals and to prepare a Report explaining its choice to the Assembly.

COUNCIL OF EUROPE
CONSEIL DE L' EUROPE

Strasbourg, 15th October, 1951.

Restricted
AS/RPP (3) 13

CONSULTATIVE ASSEMBLY

COMMITTEE ON RULES OF PROCEDURE AND PRIVILEGES

European Flag

Memorandum by the Secretariat-General

I. At a meeting held in London on 26th July, the question of a flag for the Council of Europe was submitted for consideration by the Sub-Committee.

II. The Sub-Committee agreed that this problem should be included in its agenda and that a draft Convention should be prepared for submission to the Committee of Ministers with a view to establishing the design of the flag, the conditions governing its use and the measures to be taken for its protection.

III. In the face of the numerous designs presented by the Secretariat-General, or submitted by private individuals, the Sub-Committee requested the Secretariat to make an initial selection, to arrange for the printing of some of the designs and submit them to the Committee with a view ultimately to ascertaining the views of the Assembly thereon. The designs accordingly selected have been circulated with this memorandum and a sufficient number of copies of them have been printed for distribution to the Assembly in such form and at such time as the Committee may decide.

IV. The designs should be considered in the light of the following observations:

Proposal 1

Flag of the European Parliamentary Union and Pan-European Movement. Count Coudenhove-Kalergi, in an official letter, proposed this flag on behalf of the European Parliamentary Union.

He later verbally expressed his intention of withdrawing his proposal.

./.

A 6664

Proposal 2

The green cross on a white background, which will be found
in proposal 4, is opposed by those who consider that a flag with
a predominantly white background is too easily soiled and who
submit proposal 2 in its place.

Prince Schwarzenberg proposed the same general design, but
with a yellow cross on a red background, being a reproduction
of the labarum of Constantine. Finally, a member of the staff
of the Secretariat-General has proposed a green standard (as
presented by Pope Leo III to Charlemagne at the latter's coronation),
bearing a red cross (representing the blood shed in fratricidal
struggles) superimposed on a yellow cross (emblem of the Christian
world and of the Vatican).

Proposal 3.

When verbally expressing his intention of withdrawing his
proposal (1), Count Coudenhove-Kalergi put forward proposal 3,
in effect the Cross of St. George, which has since the First
Crusade been the flag of England.

Proposal 4

A white background, symbol of purity and peace and the
emblem of authority, bears a green cross, Christian symbol of hope
and youth, which suggests at the same time the meeting at
Strasbourg of the main European highways. Green and white have
been the colours of the European Movement since its inception.
It has been suggested that the inclusion of the Strasbourg coat
of arms in the centre of the cross be restricted to the flags of
leading personalities of the Assembly, the Committee of Ministers
and the Secretariat-General. The ordinary flag would therefore
consist only of a green cross on a white background. It might
constitute the basis of a series of flags, which the Specialised
Authorities and other institutions sponsored by the Council of
Europe might be authorised to use with an appropriate distinguishing
emblem superimposed.

Proposal 5

The green and white adopted by the European Movement are
retained. The Cross of St. Andrew is included as representing
one of the oldest and most popular European emblems which has
appeared in the case of the Cross of Burgundy, emblem of the
"Grand Duchy of the West".

./.

Proposal 6

The various colours appear in the proportion in which they exist in the flags of Member States of the Council, with the white and red triangle representing the colours of Strasbourg.

Proposal 7

The United Europe flag is shown so to speak "the opposite way round" to the flag of the United States of America. The number of stars corresponds to the number of Member States.

Proposal 8

This symbol is used in the International code of signals for merchant shipping to represent the letter "E". The colours are blue and red which can be held to symbolise the conservative and progressive trends represented in the European Parliaments.

Proposal 9

The star in a circle was in 1944-45 the insignia of the armies of Liberation.

Proposal 10

The author has sought to design a "European Cross", to take its place with the Cross of Lorraine, the Maltese Cross, etc.

Proposal 11

The red background represents progress, the hand fidelity and the sun justice and hope

Proposal 12

The green and blue have the symbolic meaning stated above. The number of stars corresponds to the number of the Member States of the Council.

2191

1094

185

6 FEV. 1952

I
PL/SD

Cher Monsieur de Madariaga,

A l'occasion d'un cours que je viens de donner au
Collège de Bruges, Henri Brugmans m'avait montré votre projet.
J'ai été d'autant plus heureux de trouver votre lettre en
rentrant à Strasbourg.

Je me suis attaché au problème du drapeau européen dès
le début de mon activité au Conseil de l'Europe. J'avais
moi-même un projet qui était la croix du type scandinave
verte sur fond blanc, avec éventuellement les armes de
Strasbourg (d'argent à bandes de gueule) en coeur.

J'ai eu quelques difficultés à faire admettre aux
autorités de l'Assemblée qu'il s'agissant d'un problème vraiment
important. J'ai enfin réussi cependant à y intéresser la
Commission du Règlement et des Privilèges qui, lors de ses
dernières réunions, a décidé de soumettre à l'Assemblée une
sélection des très nombreux projets que j'avais reçus. Je vous
en fais envoyer une collection à titre d'information.

Je trouve votre proposition extrêmement intéressante.
La seule critique qui me paraisse pouvoir être retenue est
que ce drapeau qui de loin apparaît comme un drapeau bleu,
uniforme, est en fait extrêmement difficile à reproduire.
Je crois qu'il faut éviter l'écueil du drapeau des Nations-
Unies qui ne peut être fabriqué par des particuliers, et qui,
dès lors, perd beaucoup en popularité.

Si vous pouviez m'envoyer 250 exemplaires de votre
projet, je le distribuerais aux membres titulaires et suppléants
de l'Assemblée Consultative, en même temps que je leur ferais
connaître les résultats du referendum fait au cours de la dernière
session.

Je vous remercie encore et vous prie d'agréer, mon
cher Monsieur de Madariaga, à mes sentiments les meilleurs et les
plus dévoués.

                              Paul M.G. LEVY

                       Directeur de l'Information   ../..

CONSEIL DE L'EUROPE

SECRÉTARIAT GÉNÉRAL

Prière d'adresser le courrier officiel:
SECRÉTAIRE GÉNÉRAL, ou bien SECRÉTARIAT GÉNÉRAL
Please address official correspondance to the:
SECRETARY-GENERAL, or SECRETARIAT-GENERAL

Adresse télégraphique: EUROPA Strasbourg
Telegraphic address: EUROPA Strasbourg
Téléphone 534.00 à 09

COUNCIL OF EUROPE

SECRETARIAT-GENERAL

No A. 1410

15th February 1952

Sir,

<u>Emblem of the Council of Europe</u>

At the request of the Committee on Rules of Procedure and Privileges a referendum was held among all Representatives during the last few days of the Third Session of the Assembly on various proposals put forward for an emblem of the Council of Europe.

The results of this referendum are as follows:

48 Representatives have so far returned the questionnaire submitted to them.

Of these 48 Representatives, 2 rejected all the proposals submitted, 16 favoured one only and 14 placed the twelve proposals in order of preference as requested.

23 of the 48 replies - that is, nearly half - gave first preference to <u>Proposal No.1</u>: the flag of Count Coudenhove, on a field azure a gold sun bearing a cross gules. This proposal also came second twice, third twice, fifth once, sixth once, tenth once and eleventh once.

Among the comments and suggestions made about this proposal, the following should be noted:

a) No emblem of an institution of which Moslems are members may bear a cross. (Comment of a Turkish and a British Representative).

b) The general design could be retained with the addition of a crescent in the upper left-hand quarter when the emblem is used in Moslem countries;

c) Both the sun and the cross should be placed in the upper left-hand quarter;

d) The cross might extend to the edges of the flag in both directions.

A.7642
TG.726/VT/NB.

./.

The proposal obtaining the second largest number of votes was No.7 (the reverse of the American flag). It came first 9 times, second 6 times, third twice, fourth once, fifth once, seventh 3 times, eighth, ninth and tenth once each.

Among the comments on this proposal the following may be noted:

a) It is too American;

b) It is good because it is American;

c) The barry should consist of 10 pieces instead of 13.

Other proposals given first preference were as follows:

No. 2 5 times.
No. 3 twice.
No. 5 once.
No. 9 once.
No.10 twice.
No.11 once.
No.12 twice.

Among the general comments accompanying the replies the following are worthy of note:

a) Green is not a good colour since it quickly fades;

b) Only the Coudenhove proposal is possible;

c) Only Proposals 2 and 3 (cross argent on a field vert and a cross gules on a field argent) are possible;

d) Proposal No 4 might be adopted but without the Strasbourg coat-of-arms in the centre;

e) Proposal No 11 (on a field gules a sun or, and "Europa" in gold lettering) might be adopted without the white hand (two identical replies);

f) The idea of a flag with stars only, like No.12, might be adopted but in different colours (on a field gules stars argent). This, however, is too servilely American, state two Representatives.

A. 7642   ./.

g) 4 Representatives asked for a further investigation
    into the whole problem.

I thought you would like to know the results of this
inquiry which will be submitted to the Committee on Rules of
Procedure and Privileges at its next meeting.

I am, Sir,
            Your obedient Servant,

F. CARACCIOLO.
Deputy Secretary-General
Clerk of the Assembly

A.7642

The President (continued)

Does anyone demand a roll-call?...

The Assembly will therefore vote by a show of hands...

The draft Resolution is adopted unanimously.

It will be published as No. 40.

6. Supplementary Report to the Fourth Report of the Committee of Ministers

(Debate on the Reports from the competent Committees)

THE PRESIDENT (Translation). — The next item in the Orders of the Day is the debate on the draft Reply of the Assembly to the Supplementary Report to the Fourth Report of the Committee of Ministers.

Since, however, the Reports of the Committees have not yet been distributed, this debate will be held either at the close of this afternoon's Sitting or to-morrow morning.

7. Choice of an emblem for the Consultative Assembly of the Council of Europe

(Debate on the Report of the Committee on Rules of Procedure and Privileges, Doc. 198)

THE PRESIDENT (Translation). — As M. van der Goes van Naters, Rapporteur on the question of the future status of the Saar, is not yet present, I am sure the Assembly would like to pass to the next item in the Orders of the Day, which is : the choice of an emblem for the Consultative Assembly of the Council of Europe. (Report of the Committee on Rules of Procedure and Privileges, Doc. 198.)

I call M. Bichet, Rapporteur.

M. BICHET (*France*) (Translation). — Most European peoples instinctively feel that Europe will perish if it remains divided into small units, whereas unity will make it powerful and prosperous, and guarantee a peace based on the respect of liberty and justice. But these peoples need to see the idea of a united Europe embodied in the tangible form of an emblem.

The necessity of such an emblem became evident immediately upon the creation of the Council of Europe, in 1949. The champions of the European ideal used the flag with a green E on a white ground which was introduced by the European Movement at The Hague Congress. This improvised symbol was very popular, despite its lack of aesthetic appeal. In every country throughout Europe campaigns were organised, and various United Europe emblems were displayed side by side with the national colours on a number of public occasions, and even during national celebrations. Such campaigns probably did more than any number of meetings, more even than our own endeavours, to propagate the European idea among the general public. This vogue proved the need for such a symbol, for it is essential for an ideal to find expression in imagery, and the lack of an emblem for the Council of Europe has made itself keenly felt.

It was doubtless desirable for the European Movement to retain the emblem with which it had come into existence; but it was no less desirable for other European institutions, as and when established, to have their own emblems with which to demonstrate the reality of their existence. The Council's lack of a symbol has obliged it since 1949 to display the flags of all Member States, arranged as usual in English alphabetical order.

Not a week has passed since 1949 without the Secretariat-General of the Council receiving enquiries from organisations anxious to show their devotion to the ideas which it represents by displaying its flag; nor has a week passed without various individuals submitting more or less felicitous suggestions for such an emblem.

Early in 1950, the European Parliamentary Union suggested the adoption of its own flag— a golden sun with a cross gules on a field azure.

When, soon after our first Session, the Committee on General Affairs asked the Secretariat-General to draw up a report on practical steps to make public opinion more directly aware of the reality of European union, the first step suggested was the adoption of a symbol.

On 18th August, 1950, this proposal was submitted to the Assembly, which decided to refer it to its appropriate Committees, and so the question of the emblem was first referred to the Committee on Rules of Procedure and

M. Bichet (continued)

privileges. The Committee considers that the time has now come to request the Assembly to take a final decision.

Not only are the symbols of certain private associations frequently mistaken, at present, for the official emblem of the Council of Europe, but the establishment of a number of European institutions threatens to give rise to a variety of symbols, which will complicate the eventual choice of a single symbol.

We are well aware of the delicate nature of some of the necessary decisions. In the first place, it will be necessary to break away from the semi-official emblems of private movements which, whatever their merits, must give place to the official emblem of the foremost of European political institutions—that which it is the declared intention of the various Governments to adopt as the general political framework of Europe. Moreover, care must be taken to avoid regrettable manifestations of particularism, which might produce a crop of rival symbols. For instance, we have been informed that the Interim Committee of the Conference for the organisation of the European Defence Community is already considering the question of its emblem. Approaches have been made with a view to avoiding the risk of any such development.

When the Committee on Rules of Procedure and Privileges first tackled this problem, it was struck by the number of proposals that had already been made. The Secretariat-General had received over a hundred unsolicited designs from private individuals, had had the official suggestion from the European Parliamentary Union, and had itself, with the assistance of certain experts on heraldry, investigated the question of an emblem which would be satisfactory from the aesthetic, symbolic and heraldic points of view.

The designs submitted being so numerous, the Committee asked the Secretariat-General to make a preliminary selection of ten or a dozen, on which the Members of the Assembly would be asked to give an initial verdict. The Assembly was therefore consulted in December, 1951, but only one-third of its Members replied to the questionnaire. Moreover, this investigation, led to two completely contradictory results.

Among those who had expressed an opinion, there was very nearly a majority in favour of the emblem of the European Parliamentary Union, advocated by that great European pioneer, Count Coudenhove-Kalergi. But our Turkish colleagues were definitely opposed to the appearance of a cross in the emblem of the Council, and several other colleagues raised the same objection. The latter view made it impossible to adopt the flag of the Parliamentary Union and also ruled out the design prepared by the Secretariat-General—a cross vert on a field argent.

Don Salvador de Madariaga, President of the European Cultural Centre, then suggested to the Secretariat-General the adoption of a flag with a blue ground, representing the sky, and with small stars, so placed as to indicate each of our European capitals, and a larger star marking the position of Strasbourg. In practice, however, this emblem, instead of giving a clear impression of Europe, simply looked like a star-studded sky without apparent meaning.

However, the idea of stars shining in a blue firmament being acceptable the Secretariat-General finally proposed a flag having a circle of stars or on a field azure, and this was adopted by your Committee. The unbroken circle symbolises unity, whereas the stars shining in the firmament symbolise the hope of our nations.

An appropriate symbol could later be inserted in the centre of the flag of each of the European institutions. For instance, the Strasbourg Assembly could be denoted in this space by the arms of the City of Strasbourg, the European Cultural Centre by a book, and so on. These are only suggestions which should be studied in further detail. The main consideration was that agreement should be reached upon an emblem for the Consultative Assembly, which might be adopted for the Council of Europe as a whole and might also serve as a common denominator for existing or future European institutions. By preserving the general characteristics of this emblem and varying the details, these different institutions could even adopt the same basic emblem with a different central symbol representing its own particular functions, as in the examples given for the Council of Europe or the Cultural Centre.

It may be imagined that if such emblems, based on a single concept and closely related in subject, were adopted by all the countries of free Europe, they could be a very effective means of fostering the rapid and wide dissem-

M. Bichet (continued)

ination of the European idea, without which there is now no hope for our civilisation.

In view of the fact that members of the Committee have now agreed upon an emblem, it was considered unwise to embark upon a lengthy procedure before the emblem could be put into effective use. Thus, this report concludes with a Resolution and a Recommendation, of which the former must perforce be submitted to the vote before the latter. By this Resolution, the Consultative Assembly would freely decide, within the limits of its competence, to adopt as its emblem a blue flag with a circle of fifteen gold stars, which would be put into commission whenever the Assembly was in Session. The Recommendation, based on this decision of the Assembly, invites the Committee of Ministers to adopt this emblem for the Council as a whole and to take all steps to ensure that it is used widely and with appropriate dignity.

In accordance with the unanimous decision of your Committee on Rules of Procedure and Privileges, I therefore ask the Assembly to adopt the draft texts now submitted, if possible with the same unanimity.

THE PRESIDENT (Translation). — Does anyone else wish to speak?

M. ERLER (*German Federal Republic*) (Translation). — I do, Mr. President.

THE PRESIDENT (Translation). — I call M. Erler.

M. ERLER (Translation). — I have followed with sympathy the report of our Committee on Rules of Procedure and Privileges presented by M. Bichet. I am glad that a formula has been reached whereby the Council of Europe may evolve a symbol common to us all.

From the heraldic and aesthetic points of view and, considering the impression it is likely to make upon our peoples, I regard this as a good solution, but there is one matter which deserves further reflection.

The Committee proposes that we should begin by adopting this symbol for the Consult-

ative Assembly and then recommend it to the other branch of the Council of Europe, namely the Committee of Ministers. Not only is it essential that we should both have the same emblem, but I think we should also consider the political implications of this choice. The question on my mind is not without importance. True enough, the Consultative Assembly comprises delegations from fifteen Parliaments, but I recall a certain article which, while giving us all great amusement, went somewhat deeper than that by dischosing the existence of a certain political situation. This article, which discussed the arithmetics of Europe, appeared, I think, a few months ago in the Strasbourg publication, " *Revue de l'Europe* ". It demonstrated the difficuly of talking about a Europe of the Six at the same time as a Europe of the Fifteen. If one adds up the non-Member countries of the Community of the Six, one finds that there are only eight. But eight and six do not make fifteen. So we come to our problem : what about the fifteenth star?

We have always maintained that the Saar is not at the moment a State—in fact the next item in our Orders of the Day deals with just this problem—and I do not think that we can prejudice future discussions by adopting an emblem with fifteen stars, in that way recognising a hitherto non-existent State.

The idea behind the emblem is a good one, and I should like to see it accepted, but I should first like the Committee on Rules of Procedure and Privileges to consult the Committee on General Affairs on this question. We could thus find the means of establishing an emblem valid not only for the Consultative Assembly but for the whole of the Council of Europe.

I fear that political considerations well known to us all will prevent the Committee of Ministers from approving a decision of this kind by the Assembly. What we need is a common symbol for our whole institution, not only for a part of it, though our Assembly may be the more important part.

Thus, Mr. President, while assuring you of our full support for the outward appearance of our common symbol, which seems to me excel-

M. Erler (continued)

lent, I would ask you to refer this particular point back to the Committee on Rules of Procedure and Privileges, so that it may seek the opinion of the Committee on General Affairs on the political implications of this debate.

THE PRESIDENT (Translation). — I call M. Braun.

M. BRAUN (*Saar*) (Translation). — Mr. President, I hope that this statement by M. Erler is not a foretaste of our next debate. One has only to walk out of this building and count the flags outside in order to realise that the number is fifteen. No one has yet demanded the removal of one of these flags, and I see no reason for altering the emblem. If, however, you insist on doing something, I suggest the insertion of a dot with a star above it, but a somewhat dim star which would not gleam like the others (*Laughter*). Seriously, however, there must be fifteen stars, and the fifteenth should be allowed to gleam, for it does not imply recognition of the Saar as a State : our flag is not a legal argument.

THE PRESIDENT (Translation). — I call M. Bichet.

M. BICHET (*France*) (Translation). — Mr. President, I would recall that the texts submitted include a draft Resolution and a Recommendation, and that this very distinction may enable our colleague to gain full satisfaction.

How so? Nobody, not even he, would deny, I think, that there are fifteen of us here and that the flag of the Council of Europe should therefore have fifteen stars. As M. Braun pointed out just now, a visit to the entrance of the House of Europe will show that there are fifteen flags flying, and nobody has ever objected to them.

We are making a recommendation to the Committee of Ministers, and it is a matter for this body alone to amend our proposals, although their decision will make no difference to the nature of our emblem, based as it is on the principle of a fixed field and a variable number of stars. Soon, we hope, the European Coal and Steel Community and the European Defence Community will be adopting a smaller number of stars. It is for us to make a recommen-

dation and for the Committee of Ministers to size it up, interpret it and make a final decision.

Thus, at this stage, I see no difficulty so far as the Assembly is concerned. We are all agreed upon this aspect. As for the other, we are making a recommendation which we think will be adopted by the Committee of Ministers, but the latter is better qualified to weigh up the political implications of its decision.

I therefore request the Assembly to record its vote without further delay.

THE PRESIDENT (Translation). — I call M. Erler.

M. ERLER (*German Federal Republic*) (Translation). — In that case, Mr. President, I greatly fear that we shall only have an emblem for the Assembly, which I do not regard as an advantage. What we need is an emblem for the Council of Europe.

THE PRESIDENT (Translation). — Does anyone else wish to speak?...

It has been moved that the question be referred back to the Committee. I now put this motion to the vote.

I would recall that, in accordance with Article 32, paragraph 4 of the Rules of Procedure, the vote on procedural motions must be taken by sitting and standing.

I shall now ask the Assembly to vote on the motion to refer this question back to the Committee...

The motion is rejected.

I shall now ask the Assembly to vote by roll-call on the draft Resolution proposed by the Committee, which I shall now read out :

" The Consultative Assembly

1. Resolves to take as its emblem an azure flag bearing a circle of fifteen stars or (on an azure ground a circle of five-pointed stars or, none of which are touching).

2. This flag shall be flown outside the buildings of the Council of Europe whenever the Assembly is in Session.

3. Its use on other occasions shall be determined later by the Bureau of the Consultative Assembly. "

The roll-call will begin with the name of M. Müller.

Voting is open.

(*A vote by roll-call was taken.*)

THE PRESIDENT (Translation). — Does anyone else wish to vote?...

Voting is closed.

The result of the vote is as follows :

    Number of votes cast . . .　73
    Ayes . . . .　49
    Noes . . . .　17
    Abstentions . . . .　7

The draft Resolution is adopted.
It will be adopted as No. 41.
(*The list of those voting is given in Appendix II.*)

THE PRESIDENT (Translation). — The Committee further proposes a draft Recommendation, which I shall now read out :

" The Consultative Assembly,

Having adopted as its emblem an azure flag bearing a circle of fifteen stars or,

Recommends that the Committee of Ministers
(*a*) adopt the same emblem as the symbol of the Council of Europe as a whole;
(*b*) instruct the Secretary-General to enter into negotiations with the other European institutions to ensure that the emblems adopted by them shall have features similar to that adopted by the Council of Europe. "

I shall now ask the Assembly to vote on the draft Recommendation by roll-call. In the case of a draft Recommendation, it is laid down in the Rules of Procedure that the required majority is two-thirds of the votes cast by at least one-third of the Representatives.

The roll-call will begin with the name of M. Müller.

Voting is open.

(*A vote by roll-call was taken.*)

THE PRESIDENT (Translation). — Does anyone else wish to vote?...

Voting is closed.

The result of the vote is as follows :

    Number of votes cast . . .　78
    Ayes . . . .　54
    Noes . . . .　17
    Abstentions . . . .　7

The required two-thirds majority has therefore been secured.

The draft Recommendation is adopted.
It will be published as No. 56.
(*The list of those voting is given in Appendix III.*)

M. KIESINGER (*German Federal Republic*) (Translation). — May I have leave to speak?

THE PRESIDENT (Translation). — I call M. Kiesinger.

M. KIESINGER. — May I draw the attention of the Assembly to the Appendix and to the item " Symbol "? It states

" Against the sky-blue ground, the stars stand for the nations represented in the Consultative Assembly... "

I do not think that we can stick to the expression " nations ". I think that it would be better to change the text of the Appendix to conform with the text which we have accepted, and change the word " nations " to " members ".

THE PRESIDENT (Translation). — The Appendix to Doc. 198, which has been distributed, is purely an information document to complete the files of Representatives. It should be understood that the only officially valid text is the draft Resolution adopted by the Assembly.

M. KIESINGER. — I should like to point out that we really cannot use the expression " nation " for the people of the Saar. There is no Saar nation in any case.

8. *The future position of the Saar*

(Debate on the Interim Report of the Committee on General Affairs, Doc. 186)

THE PRESIDENT (Translation). — The next item in the Orders of the Day is the debate on the future position of the Saar (Debate on the Interim Report of the Committee on General Affairs, Doc. 186).

I call M. van der Goes van Naters, Rapporteur of the Committee on General Affairs.

M. VAN DER GOES VAN NATERS (*Netherlands*) (Translation). — Mr. President, Ladies and Gentlemen, the debate on the Saar follows a short politico-aesthetic debate which bears some relation to the present question, although it, naturally, settles nothing about the future status of the Saar. It also follows upon a big debate on general policy, which is only logical —since our whole future, the restoration and strengthening of Europe, the progress of the European Defence Community and Political

RESOLUTION 41 [1]

on the choice of an emblem for the Consultative Assembly
of the Council of Europe

1.   The Assembly resolves to take as its emblem an azure flag bearing a circle of fifteen stars or (on an azure ground a circle of five-pointed stars or, none of which are touching).

2.   This flag shall be flown outside the buildings of the Council of Europe whenever the Assembly is in Session.

3.   Its use on other occasions shall be determined later by the Bureau of the Consultative Assembly.

---

1. This Resolution was adopted by the Assembly at its twenty-third Sitting, on 25th September, 1953 (see Doc. 198, Report of the Committee on Rules of Procedure and Privileges).

RECOMMENDATION 56 [1]

on the choice of an emblem for the Council of Europe

The Assembly,
Having adopted as its emblem an azure flag bearing a circle of fifteen stars or,

Recommends that the Committee of Ministers
(*a*) adopt the same emblem as the symbol of the Council of Europe as a whole;

(*b*) instruct the Secretary-General to enter into negotiations with the other European institutions to ensure that the emblems adopted by them shall have features similar to that adopted by the Council of Europe.

---

1. This Recommendation was adopted by the Assembly at its twenty-third Sitting, on 25th September, 1953 (see Doc. 198, Report of the Committee on Rules of Procedure and Privileges).

V.64,136,3

DER STAATSSEKRETÄR
DES AUSWÄRTIGEN AMTS

BONN,   December 1953.

221-53 II 15802/53

Sir,

With reference to Resolution 41 of the Consultative
Assembly of 25th September regarding the choice of an
emblem for the Assembly, and to Recommendation 56 of the
Consultative Assembly of the same date with regard to the
adoption of this emblem for the Council of Europe as a
whole, I beg to draw attention to the following points :

The choice of an emblem for any one organ of the
Council of Europe such as the Consultative Assembly, is a
matter that concerns the Council as a whole. It would,
in any case, appear that the Assembly shares this view
since in Recommendation 56, it specifically recommends the
adoption of this emblem by the entire Council.

In view of the importance to be attributed to an
emblem of any kind which is the symbol of a political
organ, such a matter should be settled in an orderly
fashion. Under Articles 13 and 16 of the Statute of the
Council of Europe, the Committee of Ministers is the organ
competent to consider and propose any action required to
further the aim of the Council of Europe. This applies
more particularly to any matter of a specifically political
character, which is certainly the case where the choice of
an emblem for a part or the whole of the Council of Europe
is concerned. The choice of such an emblem is, at any rate,
a matter relating to the internal organisation and arrange-
ments of the Council of Europe, and this, under Article 16,
para. 1 of the Statute, falls within the sole competence
of the Committee of Ministers. The relevant decisions of
the Consultative Assembly therefore encroach upon the
statutory powers of the Committee of Ministers.

M. Léon MARCHAL

Secretary-General,
Council of Europe,

STRASBOURG

./.

15.462

The Federal Government thus considers that the adoption
of a special emblem for the Consultative Assembly is open
to certain objections, particularly in view of the fact that
the Member Governments of the Council of Europe have not so
far consulted each other as to whether the adoption of an
emblem for the Council of Europe would not demand a prior
addition to its Statute.

Only after some light has been shed on this matter
can the question of the form this emblem should assume be
submitted to the Committee of Ministers for discussion.

I am, Sir,
Your obedient Servant,

(signed: HALLSTEIN)

COUNCIL OF EUROPE
CONSEIL DE L'EUROPE

COMMITTEE OF MINISTERS
14th Session

Strasbourg, 19th March, 1954.

Secret
CM (54) 48
Or.Fr.

NINETEENTH MEETING OF THE MINISTERS' DEPUTIES

MEMORANDUM BY THE SECRETARIAT-GENERAL ON THE
CHOICE OF AN EMBLEM FOR THE COUNCIL OF EUROPE

PART I

Legal opinion on the powers of the two organs
of the Council in this matter

1. In the course of its Fifth Session, 1953, the Consultative Assembly adopted a Resolution and a Recommendation concerning the choice of an emblem, worded as
follows:

    (a) "Resolution (53) 41 on the choice of an emblem
       for the Consultative Assembly of the Council of
       Europe.

       "(i)   The Assembly resolves to take as its em-
            blem an azure flag bearing a circle of
            fifteen stars or (on an azure ground a
            circle of five-pointed stars or, none of
            which are touching).

       "(ii)   This flag shall be flown outside the
            buildings of the Council of Europe when-
            ever the Assembly is in session.

       "(iii) Its use on other occasions shall be de-
            termined later by the Bureau of the Con-
            sultative Assembly."

    (b) "Recommendation (53) 56 on the choice of an em-
       blem for the Council of Europe.

./.

A.16,354
TX.443/WM/NB

"The Assembly,

"Having adopted as its emblem an azure flag bearing a
circle of fifteen stars or,

"Reccomends that the Committee of Ministers:

(a) adopt the same emblem as the symbol of the Council
     of Europe as a whole;

(b) instruct the Secretary-General to enter into nego-
     tiations with the other European institutions to
     ensure that the emblems adopted by them shall
     have features similar to that adopted by the
     Council of Europe."

2.   In a letter dated 1953, M. Hallstein, Secretary of State,
pointed out to the Secretary-General of the Council of Europe
that the power to adopt a Council of Europe emblem lay solely
with the Committee of Ministers.   In support of this view,
M. Hallstein drew attention to Articles 13 to 16 of the
Statute, and more especially to the provisions of Article
15 (a) which require that "the Committee of Ministers shall
consider the action required to further the aim of the Council
of Europe ...." and to Article 16, which provides that "the
Committee of Ministers shall ... decide with binding effect,
all matters relating to the internal organisation and arrange-
ments of the Council ..".

o   o

o

3.   Before proceeding to consider the powers of the two
organs of the Council of Europe in this matter, it should be
made clear what is meant by an "emblem".

4.   An emblem should not be confused with a flag, which is
an official sign of sovereignty and sometimes of international
authority.

An emblem is merely an outward and symbolical sign by
means of which a person shows that he (or she) belongs to a
group, whether unorganised or not, or by means of which a
group displays its individuality.

./.

5.   The question now arises whether the Assembly adopted a flag or an emblem.

There are some grounds for uncertainty, since in both the Resolution and the Recommendation the word "flag" occurs.

It does not, however, appear that the Assembly adopted a flag.   The title of both the Resolution and Recommendation contains only the word "emblem".   Moreover, the substantive text of both documents states: "The Assembly resolves to take as its emblem ..." (Resolution);   "Recommends that the Committee of Ministers adopt the same emblem as the symbol ..." (Recommendation).

That an emblem is referred to, and not a flag, is confirmed by the use of the word "symbol".   The word "flag" used in the Recommendation and Resolution merely indicates the form the emblem should take.   The debates which have taken place in the Assembly bear this out.   (Official Reports, Vol. V. 1953, pp. 663 to 667).

6.   It is therefore clear that the Assembly adopted an emblem, but an emblem for the Assembly and not, for the time being, for the Council of Europe.   It is, moreover, clear that only the Committee of Ministers, as the executive organ of the Council (Article 13 of the Statute), could have adopted an emblem for the Council as a whole.

7.   The question therefore arises whether, under the Statute, the Consultative Assembly may adopt an emblem which is not at the same time that of the Council of Europe as such.

8.   In the Preamble to the Statute the Council of Europe is described as "consisting of a Committee of representatives of Governments and of a Consultative Assembly".   This definition stresses the indivisible character of the Council.   The two organs comprising the Council do not exist independently of each other, but together form a single entity.   They are served by a common Secretariat.

9.   Only the Council possesses juridical personality; its individual institutions do not (Article 1 of the General Agreement on Privileges and Immunities).

10.   The preparatory work on the Statute supported cohesion between the Committee of Ministers and the Assembly.   At the Ambassadors' Conference (London 28th March to 12th April, 1949), stress was laid upon the need for close co-operation between the two organs and it was resolved that the members of the

./.

Committee of Ministers should have the right to make recommendations to the Assembly so that both institutions might be closely associated with each other and the Committee of Ministers enabled to guide the Assembly along the desired lines (C.E. (Prep.) M. 3rd meeting, No. 4 - revised).   At the Conference of Ministers for Foreign Affairs (London, 3rd to 5th May, 1949), it was stressed that the organisation formed a single entity and that the Committee of Ministers was the key institution of the Council.

11.   It is therefore difficult to conceive that one of the institutions of the Council should be able to adopt an emblem which is not at the same time that of the organisation as a whole.

12.   It is true that the Assembly has recommended that the Committee of Ministers should adopt the same emblem for the Council as a whole, but it should be noted in this connection that the precise powers of the Assembly are laid down in the Statute.   As a general rule the Assembly may make recommendations upon any matter within the aim and scope of the Council (Article 23).   It may appoint Committees or Commissions to consider and report to it on any matter falling within its competence, to examine and prepare questions on its Agenda and to advise on all matters of procedure (Article 24). It may adopt its Rules of Procedure (Article 28), Resolutions on questions of procedure and rules governing such procedure (Articles 29 and 30).   Although the powers enumerated above may not be restrictive, the consultative character of the Assembly imposes upon it certain obligations towards the Committee of Ministers.   Generally speaking, Assembly Resolutions should not prejudice the decisions which the Ministers may be called upon to take on proposals concerning the Council of Europe as a whole.

13.   One last point is worthy of mention.   In the Assembly's Resolution No. 41 it was resolved that the flag should be flown "outside the buildings of the Council of Europe whenever the Assembly is in Session".   This order could in fact be carried out only through the Secretary-General of the Council of Europe, who is himself responsible to the Committee of Ministers under the terms of Article 37 of the Statute.

o   o

o

./.

PART II

The developments which led to the adoption of
Recommendation 56 and Resolution 41

1.   As soon as the Council of Europe came into being numerous
enquiries were received as to the nature of the Council's emblem.
Sometimes the emblems of unofficial movements were taken for
official emblems. A number of spontaneous proposals were also
made.

2.   The matter was brought to the knowledge of the Bureau of
the Assembly by the Secretary-General at the end of 1949, when
the Bureau took the view that the opinion of the Assembly as a
whole should be obtained and that a sub-committee might be
appointed to prepare a report on the matter.

3.   At the beginning of 1950 the European Parliamentary Union
proposed to the Secretary-General that the emblem of the Pan-
European Movement should be adopted.

4.   On 23rd June, 1950, the Committee on General Affairs
requested the Secretary-General to draw up a Report on the
practical steps which might be taken to make public opinion
directly aware of the reality of European union. This Report
was prepared and submitted to the Assembly as Appendix II to
Document AS (2) 85.

5.   On 18th August, 1950, the Consultative Assembly confirmed
the Resolution of the Committee of General Affairs and on 28th
August it requested each of its committees concerned to consider
the suggestions contained in the document of the Secretariat-
General. The first of these proposals concerned a "European
flag" and was referred to the Committee on Rules of Procedure
and Privileges.

6.   In the meantime a proposal by M. Bichet, Representative
to the Consultative Assembly, was laid before the French National
Assembly, requesting that the emblem of the European Movement
be flown on French Public buildings and campaigns were held for
the use of the emblem of the European Movement.

7.   On 26th July, 1951, the Sub-Committee on Immunities of the
Committee on Rules of Procedure and Privileges studied the Report
drawn up by the Secretariat-General (AS/RPP II (3) 2) and

./.

<u>resolved</u> that

    (a) in principle it was desirable that the Council
         of Europe should have its own flag and emblem;

    (b) The Secretariat-General was invited to prepare
         a Memorandum summarising the suggestions made
         for an emblem, the rules which should govern its
         use and the legislative measures necessary to
         ensure that it would receive the respect generally
         accorded to national flags.

8.   On 27th November, 1951, a plenary meeting of the Committee
on Rules of Procedure and Privileges considered the question
and resolved to seek the opinion of Representatives before itself
considering what form the emblems should take.

9.   In accordance with the Committee's instructions enquiries
were instituted among Representatives to the Assembly and the
results notified by the Clerk to the Assembly in a letter dated
13th February, 1952. 48 Representatives replied, of whom 23
said that they were in favour of the emblem of the Pan-European
Movement. A number of objections of principle were, however,
raised to the latter emblem owing to the fact that it contained
a cross.

10. Don Salvador de Madariaga, Chairman of the European Culture
Centre, proposed a flag with gold stars on a blue ground and
asked that his proposal be submitted to the Assembly.

11. On 30th August, 1952, the Europa-Union, Hamburg, gave
favourable consideration to several proposals submitted in
connection with a public competition and including one for a
blue flag with a circle of gold stars.

12. The Committee on Rules of Procedure and privileges requested
the Secretariat-General to submit a further report, but owing
to pressure of other work the Committee was unable to consider the
Report (AS/RPP (5) 1 until May, 1953. At a meeting held on 20th
May the Committee gave its provisional general approval to a
proposal for a flag comprising a circle of gold stars on an azure
ground. It resolved to consult the High Authority of the E.C.S.C.
and the Interim Commission of the E.D.C. M. Bichet was appointed
Rapporteur.

13. The unofficial consultation requested by the Committee took
place. The High Authority stated that, in principle, it was not
prepared to adopt an emblem so long as there was no Political
Community, but that it would adopt the flag of that Community

                                                              ./.

when the latter was constituted. With regard to the E.D.C., it
was confidentially stated that its Military Committee had
already adopted the white flag bearing the triple-pale green
"E" of the European Movement.

14.   On 17th September, 1953, M. Bichet presented his Report
to the Committee and, while not abandoning the first proposal
entertained by the Committee, he said that it was preferable
to revert to white and green. He tabled a draft Recommendation
calling for the adoption of the emblem by the Assembly and a
Recommendation that the Committee of Ministers should invite
Members to adopt this common emblem. The Committee decided to
retain the colours blue and gold approved by it in May and
instructed M. Bichet to prepare the final text of his Report.

15.   On 18th September, 1953, the Assembly resolved to place
the matter on its Agenda.

16.   On 21st September, M. Bichet tabled his Report (Doc. 198
of the Fifth Ordinary Session) containing a draft Resolution
and a draft Recommendation. He stated that this procedure
was suggested since it appeared "unwise to embark upon a
lengthy procedure before the emblem could be put into effective
use". It was indeed the fact that other organisations might
adopt emblems having no similarity to that of the Council which
prompted the Committee to precipitate matters; this preoccupa-
tion was clearly apparent in sub-paragraph (b). In describing
the emblem the Rapporteur moreover refrained from speaking of
"Members of the Council of Europe" prefering the words "nations
represented in the Consultative Assembly".

17.   On 25th September the matter came up for discussion in
plenary Session. After a report by M. Bichet, M. Erler,
drew the Assembly's attention to the difficulties with which
the proposal might meet in the Committee of Ministers and he
requested that it be referred to the Committee on General Afairs
for opinion. This proposal was opposed by M. Braun and the
Rapporteur, the latter pointing out that whatever the Assembly
might decide, the final decision would rest with the Committee
of Ministers, which would have "to size it up, interpret it
and make a final decision" and was "better qualified to weigh
up the political implications of its decision". The proposal
that the matter should be referred back to the Committee was
rejected. The Resolution was adopted by 49 votes to 17, with
8 abstentions, and the Recommendation by 54 votes to 17, with
7 abstentions.

18.   At the request of M. Kiesinger, the symbolic description
of the emblem was amended and the word "nations" replaced by
the word "Members".

./.

19. At a meeting of the Bureau of the Assembly on 16th
January, 1954, the Chairman expressed the view that,
having regard to certain objections raised by the German
Government, the Bureau should consider the matter as
soon as the Committee of Ministers laid it before them.

./.

PART III

Possibilities of organising a public ompetition

1.   The Secretariat-General asked the United Nations and NATO how they had chosen their respective emblems.

U.N. replied that its emblem was chosen in 1945 at the time of the San Francisco Conference and adopted by the General Assembly on 7th December, 1946. No competition had been held.

NATO also chose its emblem without holding a competition. A Committee of members of the staff of NATO had previously made a preliminary selection from among a number of suggestions and proposals from SHAPE and members of the staff of NATO. The Secretary-General, in consultation with that Committee, subsequently approved a design which was later adopted by the Permanent Representatives of the Member States of NATO.

2.   So far as the Secretariat-General is aware, no European or international organisation has chosen its emblem as the result of a competition. It is, however, a frequent practice among business undertakings to hold such competitions for the purpose of obtaining advertising slogans.

3.   Should it eventually be decided to hold a public competition for the purpose of acquiring a suitable emblem for the Council of Europe, it would be desirable first of all to insert appropriate notices in the leading newspapers of Member countries, inviting prospective competitors to submit their proposals to the Secretariat-General by a prescribed date.

Replies received would be screened and sorted by the Secretariat-General.

The replies should then be considered by a jury, which would award prizes provided for the purpose and make recommendations. The latter would be submitted to the Consultative Assembly for opinion.

A final decision would be taken by the Committee of Ministers on the basis of those recommendations and opinion.

Special credit would have to be made available to meet the costs of press publicity and for the payment of jury fees and the cost of the prizes to be awarded.

./.

4.   This procedure therefore appears to entail considerable
expense. It would also have the disadvantage of being somewhat protracted, whereas it would seem to be advisable not to
prolong the situation which arose after the adoption by the
Assembly of its Resolution No. 41 of 25th September, 1953.

RÉSOLUTION (55) **32** :   (9 décembre 1955) — *(Adoptée par les Délégués des Ministres)*

Emblème du Conseil de l'Europe

Le Comité des Ministres,

Ayant pris connaissance de la Recommandation 88 adoptée à l'unanimité par l'Assemblée Consultative le 25 octobre 1955,

Décide d'adopter, pour le Conseil de l'Europe, un emblème d'azur à un cercle composé de douze étoiles d'or à cinq rais, dont les pointes ne se touchent pas. L'emblème est conforme aux descriptions et au modèle annexés.

Description héraldique

D'azur à un cercle composé de douze étoiles d'or à cinq rais dont les pointes ne se touchent pas.

Description symbolique

Sur le fond bleu du ciel d'Occident, les étoiles figurant les peuples d'Europe forment le cercle en forme d'union. Elles sont au nombre invariable de douze, symbole de la perfection et de la plénitude.

Description géométrique

L'emblème est constitué par un rectangle bleu dont le battant (B) a une fois et demie la longueur du guindant (G). Les douze étoiles d'or s'alignent régulièrement le long d'un cercle non apparent dont le centre est situé au point de rencontre des diagonales du rectangle. Le rayon de ce cercle (R) est égal au tiers de la hauteur du guindant. Chacune des étoiles à cinq branches est construite dans un cercle non apparent, dont le rayon (r) est égal à 1/18 de la hauteur du guindant. Toutes les étoiles sont disposées verticalement, c'est-à-dire avec une branche dirigée vers le haut et deux branches s'appuyant sur une ligne non apparente, perpendiculaire à la hampe.

Les étoiles sont disposées comme les heures sur le cadran d'une montre. Leur nombre est invariable.

L'azur héraldique est représenté par le bleu outremer clair.

L'or héraldique est représenté par le jaune de chrome foncé.

THIRTY-SIXTH MEETING OF THE MINISTERS' DEPUTIES

Paris, 7th - 9th December, 1955

RESOLUTION (55) 32 :   (9th December, 1955) — *(Adopted by the Ministers' Deputies)*

Emblem of the Council of Europe

The Committee of Ministers,

Having taken note of Recommendation 88 adopted unanimously by the Consultative Assembly on 25th October, 1955,

Decides to adopt for the Council of Europe the following emblem : on a field azure a circle of twelve mullets or, their points not touching. The emblem is in accordance with the descriptions and the design attached.

Heraldic description

On a field azure a circle of twelve mullets or their points not touching.

Symbolical description

Against the blue sky of the Western world, the stars symbolise the peoples of Europe in the form of a circle, the sign of union. The number of stars is invariably twelve, the figure twelve being the symbol of perfection and entirety.

Geometrical description

The emblem is in the form of a blue rectangular flag of which the fly (F) is one and a half times the length of the hoist (H). Twelve gold stars situated at equal intervals form an undefined circle of which the centre is the point of intersection of the diagonals of the rectangle. The radius (R) of the circle is equal to one-third of the height of the hoist. Each of the stars has five points which are situated on the circumference of an undefined circle of which the radius (r) is equal to one-eighteenth of the height of the hoist. All stars are upright — that is to say, with one point vertical at 90° and two points in a straight line at right angles with the mast.

The circle is arranged so that the stars appear in the position of the hours on the face of a clock. Their number is invariable.

The colour, heraldic azure, is represented by light ultramarine blue.

The colour heraldic or is represented by deep chrome yellow.

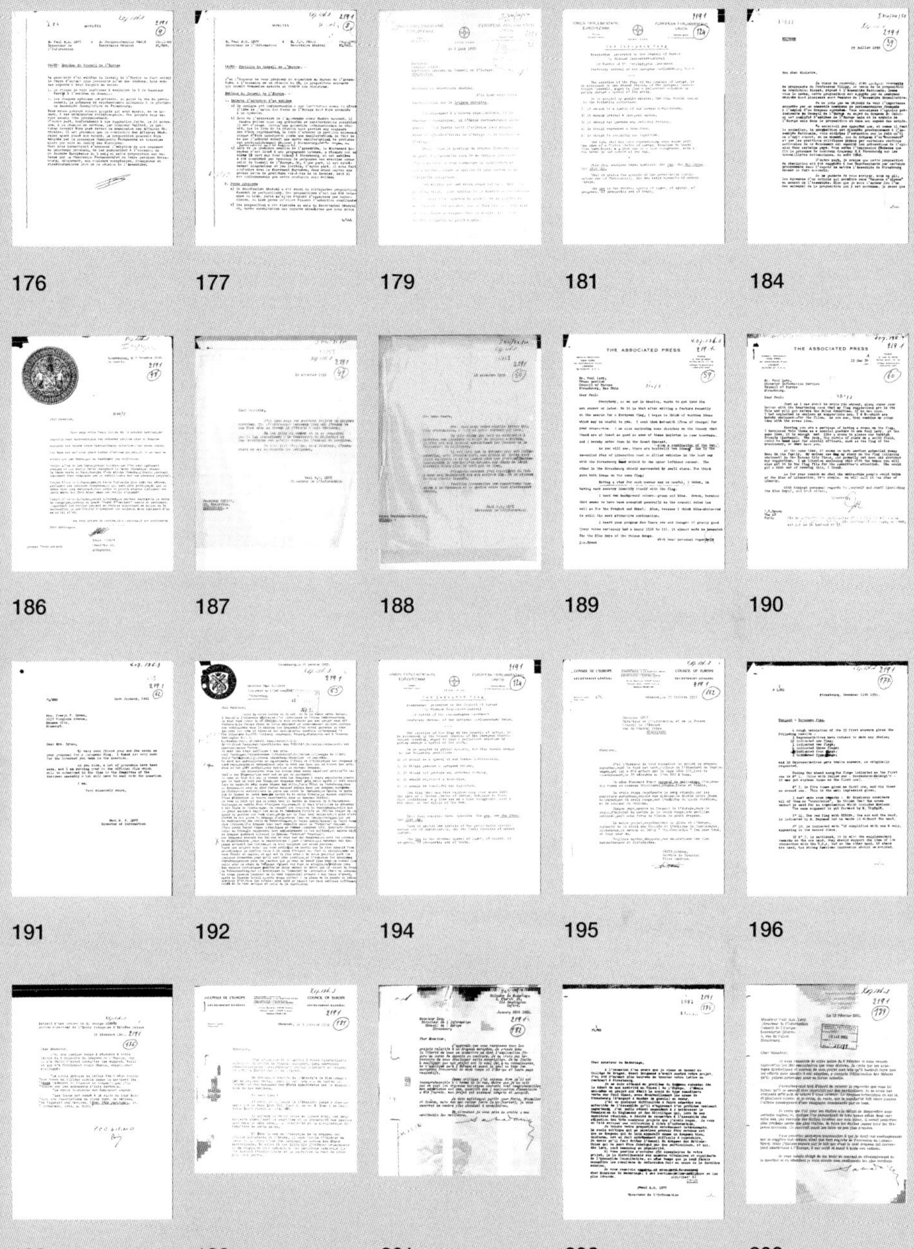

176 177 179 181 184

186 187 188 189 190

191 192 194 195 196

198 199 201 202 203

204

205

208

209

210

211

212

214

215

216

217

218

219

220

222

225

227

I 26

X09.136.3

2191

(4)

M. Paul M.G. LEVY   à   M. Jacques-Camille PARIS   23-11-49
Directeur de   Secrétaire Général   PL/GdB.
l'Information

OBJET: Emblème du Conseil de l'Europe

La nécessité d'un emblème du Conseil de l'Europe se fait sentir
de façon d'autant plus pressante qu'en son absence, nous sommes
exposés à deux dangers au moins:

1. le risque de voir continuer à assimiler le E de Monsieur
   Sandys à l'emblème du Conseil.

2. les risques spéciaux que présente, au point de vue du pavoi-
   sement, la présence de représentants allemands à la prochaine Assemblée Consultative de Strasbourg.

Nous avons préparé divers projets qui sont soumis, en ce moment, à des héraldistes strasbourgeois. Ces projets vous seront soumis très prochainement.
D'autre part, conformément à une suggestion faite, le 22 novembre, à la réunion de service, par Monsieur Halford, le problème devrait être posé devant la commission des Affaires Générales. Il est probable que la commission des Affaires Générales ayant donné son accord, la proposition pourrait être
adoptée par la prochaine Commission Permanente et transmise
alors par elle au Comité des Ministres.
Ceci nous permettrait d'annoncer l'adoption de nos couleurs
au printemps prochain, de les populariser à l'occasion de
la Journée Européenne du 5 mai (si cette proposition est retenue par la Commission Permanente) et de faire pavoiser Strasbourg, uniquement, aux couleurs européennes, françaises et
strasbourgeoises lors de la réunion de l'Assemblée.

M. Paul M.G. LEVY   à   M. J.C. PARIS   19-1-1950
Directeur de l'Information   Secrétaire Général   PL/GdB.

OBJET: Pavillon du Conseil de l'Europe. -

J'ai l'honneur de vous proposer de soumettre au Bureau de l'Assemblée, à l'occasion de sa réunion du 28, la proposition suivante
qui serait transmise ensuite au Comité des Ministres.

Emblème du Conseil de l'Europe. -

1. Raisons d'adoption d'un emblème

   a) Un emblème est indispensable à une institution comme la nôtre
      L'idée de l'union des états de l'Europe doit être attachée
      à un symbole.

   b) Lors de l'admission de l'Allemagne comme Membre associé, il
      faudra éviter tous les prétextes de manifestations possibles
      Il est d'usage, lorsqu'une Assemblée internationale se réu-
      nit, que le lieu de la réunion soit pavoisé aux couleurs
      des états représentés. Le fait d'arborer le pavillon allemand
      risque d'être interprété comme une manifestation. Le fait de
      ne pas l'arborer serait une autre manifestation. Ce problème
      est particulièrement délicat à Strasbourg. *Solution: remplacer les
      pavillons nationaux par le seul drapeau du C.E.*

   c) Lors de la première session de l'Assemblée, le Mouvement Eu-
      ropéen s'est livré à une propagande intense, a répandu son em-
      blème (E vert sur fond blanc) à Strasbourg, et cet emblème
      a été considéré par beaucoup de personnes non averties comme
      celui du Conseil de l'Europe. Or, d'une part, il est extrê-
      mement disgracieux et peu lisible, d'autre part, il nous fait
      confondre avec le Mouvement Européen. Nous avons certes une
      grosse dette de gratitude vis-à-vis de ce dernier, mais il
      est indispensable que cette confusion soit évitée.

2. Forme proposée

   a) Le Secrétariat Général a été saisi de différentes propositions
      émanant de particuliers. Ces propositions n'ont pas été rete-
      nues ou bien, parce qu'elles étaient d'apparence peu harmo-
      nieuse, ou bien parce qu'elles étaient d'exécution compliquée

   b) Une proposition a été élaborée au sein du Secrétariat Général
      et, après consultation des experts héraldistes que nous avons

∴

pu toucher, nous nous sommes arrêtés à la formule suivante:
<u>champ d'argent à croix de sinople timbrée aux armes de Strasbour</u>
En d'autres termes, un drapeau blanc portant une croix verte au
centre de laquelle se détache l'écusson de Strasbourg, écusson
blanc portant une bande transversale rouge.
<u>Le champ d'argent</u> a été choisi parce que le blanc est la couleur
qui se détache le mieux à la fois lorsque le drapeau flotte sur
les bâtiments, ou lorsqu'il flotte parmi d'autres drapeaux.
De plus, en héraldique, c'est une couleur noble et l'insigne du
commandement.
<u>La croix</u> a été choisie:
    1. Parce qu'elle se retrouve dans les drapeaux de la moitié de
       Pays membres, et c'est le seul symbole qui leur soit commun
    2. Pour symboliser la croisée des chemins.
    3. Parce qu'elle montre à la fois les directions est-ouest et
       nord-sud.
    4. Comme symbole de l'esprit chrétien.
    5. Parce qu'en héraldique, elle est à la fois le symbole le
       plus ancien et le plus noble.
<u>La couleur verte</u> de la croix a été choisie:
    1. Comme symbole d'espérance.
    2. En hommage au Mouvement Européen.
    3. Parce que c'est la seule couleur de croix non utilisée déjà
       dans un pavillon national existant.
<u>Les armes de Strasbourg</u> ont été choisies pour rappeler le siège
statutaire permanent du Conseil. En les plaçant au centre de la
croix verte, elles se détachent clairement et symbolisent Strasbourg au point de rencontre des routes européennes.

I 314/10/50.
2191
21

UNION PARLEMENTAIRE
EUROPÉENNE

Président:
GEORGES BOHY

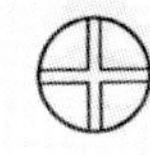

GSTAAD - SUISSE

EUROPEAN PARLIAMENTARY
UNION

Secrétaire Général:
R. COUDENHOVE-KALERGI

le 5 juin 1950

Monsieur
Camille PARIS,
Scrétaire Général du Conseil de l'Europe,
STRASBOURG.

Monsieur le Secrétaire Général,

J'ai bien reçu votre communication sur le Drapeau Européen.

Contrairement à d'autres organisations, ni le Mouvement Paneuropéen, ni l'Union Parlementaire Européenne, n'ont jamais tenté d'afficher leur drapeau comme le symbole officiel de l'Europe ou du Conseil de l'Europe.

Mais, comme la question du Drapeau Européen doit se poser à l'Assemblée lors de sa réunion plénaire, j'ai l'honneur de vous soumettre la candidature de notre emblème, comme le symbole le plus ancien de la solidarité européenne.

Cet emblème est une croix rouge sur un disque d'or: la croix rouge, comme symbole de la charité supranationale, et le disque d'or, symbole du soleil, de la lumière et de l'esprit. Cet emblème, sur un fond bleu qui symbolise le ciel, donne un drapeau beau et simple, dont vous trouvez ci-inclus un petit modèle.

./.

Ce drapeau a été utilisé par le Mouvement Paneuropéen depuis 1923 et fût adopté officiellement par l'Union Paneuropéenne lors de son premier grand Congrès, qui s'est réuni à Vienne en Octobre 1926.

Ce drapeau a aussi flotté sur les hôtels de Genève, en 1929, lors de l'Initiative Européenne d'Aristide BRIAND, Président d'Honneur de l'Union Paneuropéenne.

En décembre 1948, à l'occasion de sa réunion à Gstaad, le Conseil de l'Union Parlementaire Européenne a adopté, par unanimité, ce symbole et ce drapeau.

Au nom du Mouvement Paneuropéen, ainsi que de l'Union Parlementaire Européenne, je vous prie de bien vouloir soumettre la candidature de cet emblème et drapeau à l'Assemblée Européenne.

Veuillez agréer, Monsieur le Secrétaire Général, l'assurance de mes sentiments distingués et dévoués.

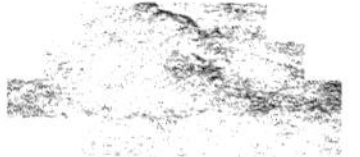

Richard Coudenhove-Kalergi.

Annexes:
1 page de la Revue Paneuropéenne de 1929,
1 drapeau,
1 petit drapeau en soie,
1 insigne de l'Union Parlementaire Européenne,
2 boutons.

UNION PARLEMENTAIRE
EUROPEENNE

Président:
GEORGES BOHY

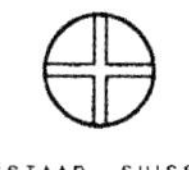

GSTAAD - SUISSE

EUROPEAN PARLIAMENTARY
UNION

Secrétaire Général:
R. COUDENHOVE-KALERGI

T h e   E u r o p e a n   F l a g

Memorandum   presented to the Council of Europe
by Richard Coudenhove-Kalergi

President of the Pan-European Mouvement

Secretary General of the European Parliamentary Union.

- - - -

The question of the flag of the Council of Europe, to
be discussed by the Second Session of the European Consultation Assembly, ought to find a definitive solution by
giving Europe a symbol of its unity.

To be adopted by public opinion, the flag should comply
to the following conditions:

1) It should be a symbol of our common civilisation;

2) It should present a European emblem;

3) It should not provoke any national rivalry;

4) It should represent a tradition,

5) It should be beautiful and dignified.

The flag that has been representing ever since 1923,
the idea of a United States of Europe, complies to these
five conditions: a golden sun on a blue background, with a
red cross in the middle of the sun.

*

This flag combines three symboles: the Sun, the Red Cross,
the Blue Sky.

Thus it unites the symbols of the greco-latin civilisation and of Christianity, the two basic elements of modern
Europe.

The Sun is the eternal symbol of light, of spirit, of
progress, of prosperity and of truth.

The Red Cross is being recogniced by the while world, by christian and non-christian nations, as a symbol of international charity and of the brotherhood of man.

The Cross has been, since the fall of the Roman Empire, the great symbol of Europe's moral unity. It is but natural that this symbol should figure within the European Flag - just as it appears on the flags of Switzerland, of Great Britain, Sweden, Norway, Danmark and other european nations.

The crushing majority of European christians will not admitt the cross being removed from the European flag - while the none-christian minority cannot oppose this symbol, inseparable from our history and civilisation; as the christian minorities in the Near East do not oppose the national symboles of the Crescant and the Star of David.

The Blue Sky, the natural background of the Sun, is a symbol of peace. Blue is bound to be the basic color of the European flag, since all other colors have at present a special meaning: the red flag = bolshevism; the green flag = islam; the yellow flag = quaran-tains; the black flag = mourning; the white flag = capitulation.

The Emblem.

Europe should have an Emblem, connected with its flag, to serve as an instrument of propaganda - as the Soviet-Star serves bolshevism and the Svastica served hitlerism.

Such a European Emblem aconstitutes the center of the flag of the U.S.E.: the red-cross on the golden (yellow) sun. Without colors, it is a cross in a circle.

This design has been found, as a pre-christian symbol of world-harmony, on celtic and germanic monuments.

National neutrality.

The flag of the U.S.E. has no national character, since it has no resemblance with any national flag. Thus it avoids the dangers of misinterpretations that would arise if letters of the alphabeth were used as elements of the European Flag. The letter E, for instance, meaning "Europe", might also be read for "England", the letter F, meaning "Federation", for "France", the letter D, meaning "Democracy", for "Deutschland", the letter U, meaning "Union", for "U.S.A." or " USSR" with all the fatal consequences of such interpretations.

Tradition.

The red cross that constitutes the center of the flag, has been undoubtedly the first European Flag at the time of the Crusades.

Combined with the sun on a blue background, it has become the most ancient symbol of the european idea. Since 1923 this flag has been adapted throughout Europe, as symbol of the Pan-European Movement. Acclaimed by the first Pan-European Congress in Vienna in 1926, this flag has floated over the roofs of Geneva, to great in 1929 the European Initiative of Aristide Briand, the Honorary Chairman of the Pan-European Union.

After the war, the European Parliamentary Union, that has launched the idea of a European Parliament elected by the national parliaments, has adopted this *flag* in December 1947, by an unanimous vote of its Council.

Beauty and Dignity.

The evident beauty and dignity of this flag have never been contested.

**

All these reasons recommend the adoption of this flag by the Council of Europe.

Should the Council choose another symbol of its present structure of an association of sovereign nations, our flag will, under all circumstances, continue to be the symbol of the struggle for a European Federation - up to the birthday of the Unites States of Europe.

Gstaad, 27 July 1950.

R. Coudenhove-Kalergi.

10631

I 314/24/50
X4.156.0
2191
(39)

EXPRESS

29 juillet 1950

Mon cher Ministre,

Je viens de recevoir, avec quelques documents de propagande du Professeur Villey, le texte de la proposition de résolution Bichet, déposé à l'Assemblée Nationale. Comme vous le savez, cette proposition est appuyée par de nombreux députés dont plusieurs sont Membres de l'Assemblée Consultative.

Je ne puis que me réjouir de voir l'importance accordée par un ensemble nombreux de parlementaires français à l'emploi d'un drapeau européen. Vous connaissez l'opinion prédominante au Conseil de l'Europe au sujet du drapeau E. Celui-ci est qualifié d'emblème de l'Europe unie et de symbole de l'Europe unie dans la proposition et dans son exposé des motifs.

Ne serait-il pas opportun que, si comme il faut le souhaiter, la proposition est discutée prochainement à l'Assemblée Nationale, vous attiriez l'attention sur le fait qu'il ne s'agit encore, en ce moment, que du drapeau d'un "Mouvement" et que les positions politiques prises par certaines sections nationales de ce Mouvement ont suscité les préventions de l'opinion dans certains pays. Vous savez l'impression fâcheuse que fit la présence de nombreux drapeaux E à Strasbourg sur les travaillistes britanniques, en août 1949.

D'autre part, je crains que cette proposition de résolution ait été suggérée à des Représentants par certains groupements dans l'espoir de mettre l'Assemblée de Strasbourg devant le fait accompli.

Je me permets de vous envoyer, sous ce pli, les épreuves d'un article qui paraîtra dans "Saisons d'Alsace" au moment de l'Assemblée. Bien que je sois l'auteur (ou l'un des auteurs) de la proposition qui y est contenue, je pense que

.../...

29 juillet 1950

./...

c'est à l'Assemblée, et à l'Assemblée seulement, qu'incombera
le soin de se prononcer et je suis bien décidé, pour ma part,
à ne pas insister si on se prononce dans un autre sens. Il est
certain pourtant que l'acceptation pure et simple du drapeau E
serait une catastrophe au moins esthétique.

Je profite de cette lettre pour vous confirmer
les requêtes que je me suis permis de vous présenter hier par
téléphone:

1. Alors que nous possédons déjà le détail des programmes d'une
   quinzaine de radios, nous ne connaissons rien encore des projets de la Radiodiffusion Française, sinon qu'elle va nous
   envoyer un reporter.

2. Pourriez-vous faire consacrer un programme de télévision
   à la réunion de l'Assemblée?

3. Le pool des actualités cinématographiques est représenté par
   Eclair-Journal. D'après Noël, il y aurait une entreprise
   nationalisée d'actualités françaises. Pourrait-on veiller
   à ce qu'elle ne nous oublie pas.

4. A la date du 28 juillet, 299 journalistes ont demandé leur
   accréditement au Conseil de l'Europe pour la prochaine Assemblée. Parmi eux, il y a 73 Britanniques (dont 27 B.B.C.),
   46 Allemands, 41 Américains et 69 Français dont 25 Périsiens
   seulement. Des Etats membres, seules la Grèce, la Turquie
   et l'Islande ne nous ont pas encore annoncé de journalistes
   (ce qui ne m'étonne d'ailleurs pas et n'offre pas d'inconvé-
   nients graves étant donné les accords passés par les agences
   de presse de ces pays avec France-Presse et Reuter).

Je m'excuse d'avoir retenu aussi longuement vo-
tre attention et je vous prie d'agréer, mon cher Ministre, l'assurance de ma très haute considération.

Monsieur Guy MOLLET,
Ministre d'Etat,
rue de Bellechasse,
Paris (7ème). -

Paul M.G. LEVY
Directeur de l'Information

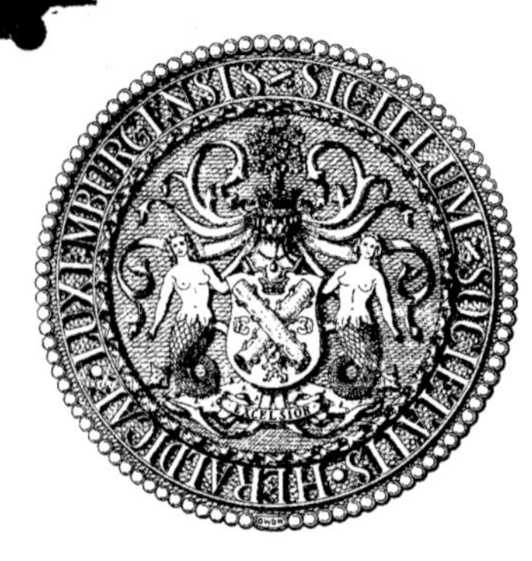

XQ.136.3
I 314/30/...

2191
(48)

9544/I

LUXEMBOURG, le 6 Novembre 1950.
22, GRAND-RUE

Cher Monsieur,

Bien reçu votre bonne lettre du 24 octobre dernier,par laquelle nous apprenons,que nos modestes projets pour un drapeau européen ont retenu votre bienveillante attention.Nous avons encore ici dans nos archives grand nombre d'autres projets,et je ne vous en envois que les trois,qui me semblent les meilleurs:

Projet A)Dessin Lex Weyer,projet L.Weyer.Que l'on peut également changer en une étoile verte chargeant la bande blanche,ou encore la bande verte en haut,chargée d'une étoile blanche.L'étoile pourrait également être remplacée par un soleil(comme sur nos premiers projets).

Projet B)Dessin L.Weyer,projet Louis Wirion.Le plus prés des vôtres, seulement aux couleurs inversées,ce qui sera plus pratique,vu que le blanc sera trop salissant.Mais enfin on pourra adopter également une croix verte sur fond blanc avec une étoile d'argent!

Projet C)Dessin L.Weyer,projet L.Wirion.Le sautoir représente la croix de Bourgogne,symbole du grand "Duché d'Occident" centre du continent. (Cependant les étoiles devront se trouver exactement au milieu de la hauteur)Ici la possibilité d'inverser les couleurs sera également d'un assez bel effet.

Nous vous prions de croire,cher Monsieur,à nos sentiemnts très distingués

Louis WIRION
Grand'Rue 22.
LUXEMBOURG.

Annexe: Trois projets

I 314/31/50

14992
Xg 156.3 2191
(49)

10 novembre 1950

Cher Monsieur,

J'ai bien reçu vos nouveaux projets de drapeau
européen. Ils m'intéressent beaucoup bien que j'avoue ne
pas être très en faveur de l'étoile à huit branches.

Je les joins au dossier et je ne manquerai
pas de les communiquer à la Commission du Règlement et
des Privilèges dès qu'elle reprendra l'examen du problème.

Je vous prie d'agréer, cher Monsieur, l'assurance de mes sentiments les meilleurs,

                              Paul M.G. LEVY
                           Directeur de l'Information

Monsieur WIRION,
22, Grand'Rue,
LUXEMBOURG. -

I 3.4/32/10
Kg. 136.3
14991
2191
50

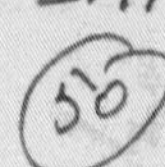

10 novembre 1950

Mon cher Comte,

J'ai bien reçu votre aimable lettre qui, pour m'atteindre, a fait un grand circuit par Rome.

Je vous avoue que tout en continuant à préparer mes dossiers au sujet du drapeau européen, je n'ai pas osé presser exagérément les Membres de la Commission du Règlement.

Il est vrai que le drapeau nous est indispensable, mais d'autre part, des choses si graves sont mises en question en ce moment même que j'estime psychologiquement la sortie d'un drapeau sur champ de néant pourrait faire plus de tort que de bien.

N'importe comment j'en reparlerai au Président van Cauwelaert dès son arrivée ici. Je me réjouis de vous revoir bientôt.

Veuillez transmettre mes respectueux hommages à la Comtesse et me croire votre bien sincèrement dévoué,

Paul M.G. LEVY
Directeur de l'Information

Comte Coudenhove-Kalergi,
GSTAAD. -

X07.136.3
219-A

THE ASSOCIATED PRESS

BUREAUX PRINCIPAUX
NEW YORK
50, ROCKEFELLER PLAZA
LONDON
85 FLEET ST., E. C. 4

PARIS
21, RUE DE BERRI
ELYsée 86-76, 77, 78
ADRESSE TÉLÉGRAPHIQUE
"ASSOCIATED PARIS"

(59)

Mr. Paul Levy,
Press section
Council of Europe
Strasbourg, Bas Rhin

364/I

Dear Paul:

Everybody, as we say in America, wants to get into the act sooner or later. So it is that after writing a feature recently on the search for a European flag, I began to think of various ideas which may be useful to you. I send them herewith (free of charge) for your inspection. I am also enclosing some sketches on the theory that these are at least as good as some of these depicted in your brochure, and I hereby enter them in the Great Contest.

As you will see, there are basically two ideas. One is the
plus a combination of the two.
so-called Star of Liberation used on Allied vehicles in the last war with the Strasbourg shield in the upper lefthand corner. The other is the Strasbourg shield surrounded by small stars. The third puts both ideas on the same flag.

Having a star for each member may be useful, I think, in having each country identify itself with the flag.

I used two background colors--green and blue. Green, because that seems to have been accepted generally as the council color (as well as for the Prophet and Hope). Blue, because I think blue-white-red is still the most attractive combination.

I heard your program New Years eve and thought it pretty good (your voice certainly had a happy lilt to it). It almost made me homesick for the Blue Boys of the Maison Rouge.

With best personal regards,

j.e.dynan

THE ASSOCIATED PRESS

BUREAUX PRINCIPAUX
NEW YORK
50, ROCKEFELLER PLAZA
LONDON
85 FLEET ST., E. C. 4.

13 Jan 50

PARIS
21, RUE DE BERRI
ELYSÉE 86-76, 77, 78
ADRESSE TÉLÉGRAPHIQUE
" ASSOCIATED PARIS "

60

Mr. Paul Levy,
Director Information Service
Council of Europe
Strasbourg.

Dear Paul:

48/I

     Just as I was about to write you anyway, along comes your letter with the heartening news that my flag suggestions are in the file and will get before the Rules Committee, if no one else. I had neglected to enclose my suggestions nos. 7 & 8--which are hereby enclosed--for the files. As you see, they combine my other idea with the cross idea.

     Knowing you are a partisan of having a cross on the flag, I developed this theme as a special gesture to one Paul Levy. At the same time, it is enough not like a cross to please our turkish friends (perhaps). The jack, the circle of stars on a solid field, could be xxxx used for special officers, such as the flag of the presidency, or what have you.

     At the same time, it seems we have another potential Betsy Ross in the family. My mother saw xxx my story on the flag (clipping enclosed) in the Kansas City Times, and promptly sat down and sketched her suggestion. I am likewise enclosing this with the hopes you will also put it in the flag file for the committee's attention. She would get a kick out of knowing this, I think.

     As for your remark on what the outre-rhin people would think of the Star of Liberation, it's simple. We will call it the Star of Liberty.

     With kindest personal regards to yourself and staff (including the Blue Boys), and best wishes,

Sincerely,

J.E.Dynan
The AP
Paris

PS: my mother's own explanation of her idea is written on the reverse of her sketch. She miscounted the rays, however, and put in 16 instead of 15.

X 07. 136.3

558

219 1

(62)

PL/MRH   18th January, 1951

Mrs. Joseph V. Dynan,
5117 Virginia Avenue,
Kansas City,
Missouri.

Dear Mrs. Dynan,

          My very good friend your son Joe sends me
your proposal for a European Flag. I thank you very much
for the interest you take in the question.

          As you know, a lot of proposals have been
made, and I am putting your in the official file which
will be submitted in due time to the Committee of the
European Assembly which will have to deal with the question.

          I am,

               Very sincerely yours,

                         Paul M. G. LEVY
                         Director of Information

Luxembourg,le 25 janvier 1951.

Xof.136.3
219 1

(65)

Monsieur Paul M.G.Lévy

Directeur de l'Information

Strasbourg.
____

CONSEIL DE L'EUROPE
COUNCIL OF EUROPE
...GENERAL
27 ... 1951
867 15

Cher Monsieur,

    Merci de votre lettre du 24 crt. et de la revue nôtre Europe,
à laquelle j'aimerais m'abonner.J'ai communiqué au Prince Schwarzenberg,
ce dont vous venez de me charger.Je suis enchanté que son projet vous ait
intéressé.Le Prince étant un homme charmant et exessivement cultivé,quoique
non spécialiée dans la science des drapeaux.Pour votre gouverne je vous
donnerai les noms et adresses des spécialistes mondiaux en"drapeaux ":
Mrs Elizabeth W.KING. National Geographic Society.Sixteenth and M Streets.
Washington D.C. 6.
H.Gresham Carr. 46.Dobell Road.London.S.E.9.
Dr Ottfried Neubecker,Schriftleiter des "HEROLD".30.Berlin-Zehlendorf-West
Amerikanischer Sektor.
Ce sont les trois meilleurs à mon avis.
Karl Fachinger.Falkenstrasse 6.Stahnsdorf.Kr.Teltow.(Allemagne de l'Est)
Roger Harmignies.135.Avenue Grandchamp.Bruxelles et moi-même.
Ce sont des spécialistes en ce concerne l'étude et l'historique des drapeaux d
tout pays,peuple,ou nation,mais cela ne veut pas dire que ce soient des arti=
stes au bon goût parfait,pour dessiner un nouveau drapeau.

    Les directives vous les donnez dans votre excellent article"La ba=
taille des Drapeaux",ce sont celles qui me guidèrent.
Je vous ai déjà dit que je trouve ,tous les drapeaux à croix excellents,pourvu
que le fond ne soit pas blanc,ces drapeaux sont gris sales après un très court
laps de temps.De même aucun blason de ville,fusse celui de Strasbourg,dans
un drapeau,et pour de plus fortes raisons encore dans une drapeau européen.
La fédération australienne ne porte pas celui de Canberra,la Suisse né porte
pas le blason de Berne dans le centre de sa croix blanche,ni aucune capitale
d'une fédération se trouve représentée dans un drapeau fédéral.
Je vous ai déjà dit que la croix dans le cercle du drapeau de M.Coudenhove-
Kallerghi,me semble être d'origine nipponne,et il veut d'ailleurs le réserver
à ses Etats de Charlemagne. On connaît une bannière de Charlmeagne,celle que
le grand empereur reçut des mains du Souverain Pontife en 800.Son projet de la
croix de gueules sur fond blanc,pêche par le fond trop salissant,et puis c'est
encore de nos jours le drapeau d'Angleterre (non de Grande-Bretagne,qui est
la combinaison des croix de Saint-Georges,de Saint André(Ecosse) de Saint Pat=
rick (Irlande)/Le drapeau tout vert rappelle celui du "Prophète" Mohomet .
(Voir Artin Yacoub Pacha -Héraldique en Orient -Londres 1902. Quaritch-Editeur
Celui au triangle représente trop exclusivement le but culturel,il existe déjà
un drapeau purement culturel le drapeau "Roerich" "mondial".
Les drapeaux portant des lettres ne sont pas des drapeaux,ce sont des poteaux
de signalisation ,vous ne rencontrerez à part l'Arabie,que rarement des dra=
peaux arborant des lettres,et ce sont toujours les moins réussis.
Parmi mes projets celui que vous publiez,ne me semble pas le plus réussi. Per=
sonnellement je préfère celui à la croix d'argent sur fond de sinople,avec ou
sans étoile au centre, et qui est le plus proche de votre projet,à part les
couleurs inversées,pour qu'il soit plus pratique,et l'omission des armoiries
strasbourgeoises pour les raisons que je vous ai donné plus haut.En second lieu
celui avec la croix de Borgogne d'argent sur fond de sinople,cet emblème pour
des raisons historiques possède au moins autant de droit que le projet du Prin
ce Schwarzenberg.Car effectivement le "Labarum" de Constantin était un morceau
de tissu pourpre (couleur de la Rome impériale) attaché à une lance d'abord,
après la fameuse bataille,cette hampe portait à la place de la pointe de lance,
un croix d'or,bien des siècles plus tard on réunit les deux emblèmes différent
celui de la Rome antique et celui de la Chrétienté.

Les raisons historiques qui plaident pour l'emblème bourguignon sont les
suivantes:
Reprenant la tradition des anciens pays centraux de l'Europe occidentale,
pays dont est issu Charles Martel,sauveur en son temps de l'Occident et le
grand empereur unificateur Charlemagne.Reprenant ensuite la tradition de la
Lotharingie,pays entre-deux,centre du Continent,la Bourgogne réunit sous cet
emblème,les Pays-Bas,la Belgique,la Flandre française,l'Artois,une parti de
la Picardie,Le Luxembourg,l'Alsace,(Strasbourg,était ville d'empire)une bonne
partie de la Lorraine,la Franche-Comté et la Bourgogne proprement dite.Si le
rêve des grand-ducs d'Odcident ce fut réalisé,si Charles le Téméraire aurait
été plus diplomate que guerrier,on aurait vu au cours des siècles se grouper
autour de ce noyau ,l'empire de plus en plus affaibli,et qui ne serait pas tom-
bé sous la coulpe des Habsbourg et et probablement malgré le génie centralisa-
teur de Louis XI,la France des Henri II ou III! Il y aurait déjà une fédération
européenne des Pyrénées aux confins de Pologne et de Hongrie,et elle aurait au
moins trois siècles d'existence et jamais on n'aurait vu les guerres fratrici=
des entre Français et Allemands,qui se sont succédés depuis le cardinal Riche=
lieu.

Vous me répondrez,que tout cela c'est de la spéculation historique.Mais
si vous lirez le livre de l'historien néerlandais Huizinga (Im Banne der Geschi
chte) et d'autres travaux d'historiens,dont celui de Luc Hommel,Luxembourgeois
habitant la Belgique -Le Grand Héritage,vous verrez le rôle formidable que les
grand-ducs bourguignons ont joué sur la scène européenne/.Mais ce qui est mieux
c'est que la tradition de cette fédération d'états européens est loin d'être
éteinte,la croix de Bourgogne vit dans le collier de la Toison d'Or que dé=
cernent les Habsbourgs,aussi bien que les Bourbon d'Espagne.L'ordre néerlandais
de Guillaume porte des emblèmes bourguignons.Partout dans l'architecture des
Flandres aux Alpes on rencontre la croix de Saint André sur les édifices les
plus divers ,on pose les armoiries de bien des pays sur la dite croix,elle
est sculptée sur des meubles,gravée sur les monnaies les plus diverses,surtout
espagnoles.Elle figurait dans les drapeaux espagnoles,formait jusqu'à la veille
de la révolution le drapeau des Provinces-Belgiques,et je pourrais continuer
ces exemples sur des vêtements,des vitraux,des faïences.....Ce ne fut pas seu=
lement un emblème centre-eurpéen,mais par les héritiers des ducs de Bourgogne
les Habsbourg d'Autriche et d'Espagne ,il rayonnait à travers l'empire,l'Italie
l'Espagne,et par les Bourguignons dans certaines contrées de France!

Je crois,que vus ces considérations il n'y aura pas d'autre emblème digne
de figurer l'Europe nouvelle,notre Europe que la croix latine,d'argent sur
fond de sinople (variante:la croix d'or du labarum de Constantin sur la pour=
pre de l'empire romain) et troisième;et selon ce qui précède la plus intéres=
sante variante la croix de Sainte André d'argent également sur un fond de sinop
le.Ce seront les drapeaux les plus simples,les plus significatifs,les plu=
symboliques et les "chantants",car ils glorifieront une tradition de plus de
deux millénaires

Je vous prie de croire,cher Monsieur,à mes sentiments les meilleurs
et les plus dévoués ————— Louis Wirion

Délégué Correspondant pour le
Grand Duché de Luxembourg
de l'A. F. C. E. L. - 22, Grand'rue
Luxembourg

P.S.
Tout ceci fut écrit en toute hâte,car je suis débordé de travail,veuillez
donc excuser les inombrables fautes de frappe.

193

Strasbourg, le 26 septembre 1951.

Objet : Drapeau européen.

D'accord pour les dessins du drapeau européen. Je précise ci-dessous les couleurs et l'ordre dans lequel les modèles doivent être numérotés.

Les numéros sont portés dans le coin inférieur gauche de chaque projet.

Pour le projet N° 7, il faudrait compléter le franc - quartier en mettant 15 étoiles d'or. Pour les couleurs, je les reprends ci-dessous afin d'éviter toute confusion;
1) drapeau bleu avec soleil jaune portant une croix rouge.
2) Drapeau rouge à croix jaune.
3) drapeau vert à croix blanche.
4) drapeau blanc à croix verte, portant les armes de Strasbourg en coeur.
5) drapeau vert à croix de St-André blanche.
6) bande bleue, vert, jaune, noir, avec triangle blanc et rouge.
7) bandes horizontales alternativement bleues et blanches, francs-quartiers rouges à étoiles d'or.
8) bande supérieure bleue, bande inférieure rouge.
9) drapeau vert, étoile et cercle blancs, armes de Strasbourg.
10) drapeau blanc, 4 E verts.
11) drapeau rouge, main blanche, Europa et soleil jaunes.
12) drapeau blanc, 15 étoiles vertes.

La présentation finale devra être faite sous forme de "cartes postales" isolées, dont chacune portera, dans le coin à choisir par vous, et très discrètement, mais très lisiblement, le numéro correspondant. Eventuellement, je verrai avec Antoine Fischer dans quelles conditions on pourrait imprimer des explications et commentaires au dos de chaque projet.

Paul M.G. LEVY
Directeur de l'Information

Monsieur Fischer.

Référence à rappeler: A/H.
Please quote :

STRASBOURG, le 15 Octobre 1951

Monsieur LEVY
Directeur de l'Information et de la Presse
Conseil de l'Europe
rue du Général Frère
STRASBOURG

Monsieur,

J'ai l'honneur de vous soumettre un projet de drapeau européen, dont le fond est vert, couleur de l'étendard de Charlemagne, qui lui a été offert par le Pape Léon III, lors du couronnement, le 25 décembre en l'An 800 à Rome.

Ce même étendard était parsemé de paillettes d'or, avec six roses ou rosaces tricolores, rouges, bleus et blancs.

La croix rouge représente le sang répandu par les guerriers européens, depuis des siècles. La double croix jaune accompagnant la croix rouge, est l'emblème du monde chrétien, et la couleur du Vatican.

Chaque pays, membre du Conseil de l'Europe, aura le choix, d'ajouter au centre de la croix rouge, son pavillon national, soit sous forme de blason ou petit drapeau.

Un autre projet, représentant le globe et l'Europe, surmonté de la croix des Croisés et l'emblème de Charlemagne, ci-dessous, la devise en latin " Vis-Concordia " (un pour tous, et tous pour un.

Veuillez agréer, Monsieur, mes salutations les plus respectueuses et distinguées.

HEITZ, Arsène,
Service du Courrier
Place Lenôtre.

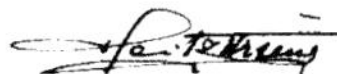

Strasbourg, December 11th 1951.

<u>Subject</u> : <u>European flag</u>.

A rough tabulation of the 33 first answers gives the following results :
    3 Representatives have refused to make any choice;
    10 indicated one flag;
    1 indicated two flags;
    4 indicated three flags;
    [illegible] indicated four flags;
    2 indicated five flags;

and 10 Representatives gave twelve answers, as originally requested.

Coming far ahead among the flags indicated as the first one is N° 1. (blue with yellow sun - Coudenhove-Kalergi's - it was put sixteen times as the first one).

N° 7. is five times given as first one, and six times as second one. This is the main impression given.

I must make some remarks : Mr Hopkinson considers all of them as "unsuitable". He thinks that the cross cannot be used for an organisation which includes Moslems. The same argument is put forward by M. Urgüplü.

N° 11. The red flag with EUROPA, the sun and the hand, is indicated by M. Reynaud but he wants it without the hand.

N° 10. is indicated with "if simplified with one E only, appearing in the second place.

If N° 7. is mentioned, it is with the supplementary remark; on the one hand, they should support the idea of its connection with the U.S.A. but on the other hand, if stars are used, too strong American impression should be avoided.

../..

When N° 4. is mentioned, it is each time with the proposed suppression of the Strasbourg coat-of-arms.

Some of the Members have suggested to study the whole matter over again (two of them).

Paul M.G. LEVY
Director of Information

Mr. HOY

Extrait d'une lettre de M. George COEDÈS
Ancien directeur de l'Ecole Française d'Extrême Orient

16 décembre 1951.

Cher Monsieur,

J'ai mis quelque temps à répondre à votre
lettre du 8 relative au drapeau de l'Europe, car
il m'a fallu d'abord consulter les augures. Voici
ce que m'a finalement remis Hambis, mongolisant
distingué:

"La croix grecque ou latine était déjà connue
"des Turcs au VIIIème siècle comme le montrent les
"tamga (marques ou figures de blason?) que l'on
"trouve sur les monuments d'Asie Centrale.
        "La croix tournante est également connue.

        "Les Turcs ont donné à la suite de leur édi-
"tion des inscriptions en vieux turc, un tableau
"où figurent ces marques. (Eski Türk yazitlari, IV,
" Istamboul, 1941, p. 210)."

Xop. 136. 3

2191.

(181)

STRASBOURG, le 5 janvier 1952

Monsieur,

J'ai l'honneur de soumettre à votre bienveillante attention un projet de drapeau européen, dont certaines caractéristiques conviendraient particulièrement au drapeau de l'Union Européenne et de l'Armée.

Ce drapeau s'inspire de l'Etendard de Charlemagne par sa couleur verte, (dont il est possible de varier la teinte) et des drapeaux des Etats Scandinaves par la disposition de ses emblèmes.

Il sera donc :

1) vert, en souvenir de l'Etendard donné à Charlemagne par le Pape Léon III, lors du sacre à Rome à la basilique Saint Pierre en l'An 800.

2) portera la croix rouge au liseré d'or, ces deux couleurs symbolisant le sacrifice et la fraternité des peuples unis dans un même idéal, la prospérité et la civilisation qui résultera de cette union.

3) Dans le cas de l'adoption de ce drapeau par l'Union Européenne et l'Armée, il sera facile d'insérer au coeur de la croix l'emblème national de chacun des Etats participants. En effet il est difficile d'éffacer brusquement et de remplacer sans transition des pavillons nationaux qui ont suscité l'enthousiasme et le sacrifice de tant de héros pour leur patrie.

Le fait d'autre part de mettre la croix figurant sur les emblèmes scandinaves,à l'étendard de Charlemagne,peut symboliser l'avènement d'une Europe plus complète que celle de l'Empire Carolingien.

Les renseignements concernant l'Etendard de Charlemagne se trouvent a la bibliothèqua Château des Rohans a Strasbourg.

Veuillez agréer,Monsieur,mes sentiments très respectueux.

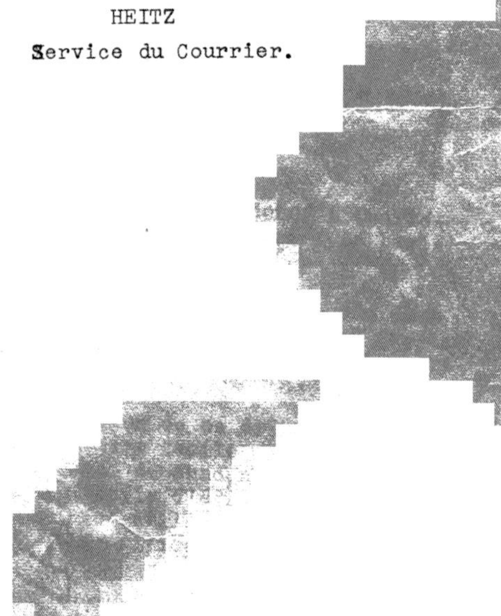

HEITZ
Service du Courrier.

Monsieur F. Caracciolo
Secrètaire Adjoint,
Greffier de l'Assemblée
Conseil de l'Europe
S T R A S B O U R G

Salvador de Madariaga
3, Church St.
Old Headington
Oxford.

January 25th 1952.

Monsieur Lévy
    Directeur de l'Information
    Conseil de l'Europe
        Strasbourg

Cher Monsieur,

        J'apprends, que vous reunissez tous les
projets relatifs à un drapeau européen. Je prends donc
la liberté de vous en soumettre un dont l'explication figure au verso du dessein en couleurs. Je ne crois pas ne-
cessaire de vous développer cette description. Je me limite
à souligner que mon projet est le seul qui, à ma connaissance,
ne s'applique qu'à l'Europe; et aussi le seul ou tous les
européens trouveront en meme temps et l'Europe et leurs pays
respectifs.

        Comme critique j'ai entendu dire qu'il est
incomprehensible à l'homme de la rue. Outre que je ne vois
pas en quoi les drapeaux nationaux courants sont comprehensibles
mon experience est que, aussitôt que l'explication elementaire
a été fournie, mon projet est aisement compris et accepté.

        Je dois maintenant partir pour Paris, Bruxelles
et Genève, mais des mon retour (vers la mi-fevrier), je vous
enverrai un nombre plus abondant d'exemplaires.

        En attendant je vous prie de croire a mes
sentiments les meilleurs.

1094   2191
(185)

6 FÉV 1952

I
PL/SD

Cher Monsieur de Madariaga,

    A l'occasion d'un cours que je viens de donner au Collège de Bruges, Henri Brugmans m'avait montré votre projet. J'ai été d'autant plus heureux de trouver votre lettre en rentrant à Strasbourg.

    Je me suis attaché au problème du drapeau européen dès le début de mon activité au Conseil de l'Europe. J'avais moi-même un projet qui était la croix du type scandinave verte sur fond blanc, avec éventuellement les armes de Strasbourg (d'argent à bandes de gueule) en coeur.

    J'ai eu quelques difficultés à faire admettre aux autorités de l'Assemblée qu'il s'agissant d'un problème vraiment important. J'ai enfin réussi cependant à y intéresser la Commission du Règlement et des Privilèges qui, lors de ses dernières réunions, a décidé de soumettre à l'Assemblée une sélection des très nombreux projets que j'avais reçus. Je vous en fais envoyer une collection à titre d'information.

    Je trouve votre proposition extrêmement intéressante. La seule critique qui me paraisse pouvoir être retenue est que ce drapeau qui de loin apparaît comme un drapeau bleu, uniforme, est en fait extrêmement difficile à reproduire. Je crois qu'il faut éviter l'écueil du drapeau des Nations-Unies qui ne peut être fabriqué par des particuliers, et qui, dès lors, perd beaucoup en popularité.

    Si vous pouviez m'envoyer 250 exemplaires de votre projet, je le distribuerais aux membres titulaires et suppléants de l'Assemblée Consultative, en même temps que je leur ferais connaître les résultats du referendum fait au cours de la dernière session.

    Je vous remercie en vous priant de croire, cher Monsieur de Madariaga, à mes sentiments les meilleurs et les plus dévoués.

Paul M.G. LEVY

Directeur de l'Information   ../..

SALVADOR DE MADARIAGA
3, CHURCH STREET,
OLD HEADINGTON,
OXFORD.

Le 13 Février 1952.

Monsieur Paul M.G. Levy
 Directeur de l'Information
Conseil de l'Europe
Secrétariat Général
5, rue du Palais
Strasbourg.

CONSEIL DE L'EUROPE
COUNCIL OF EUROPE
Secrétariat Général

1 6 FEV. 1952

Cher Monsieur,

    Je vous remercie de votre lettre du 6 Février et vous remets aujourd'hui les 250 exemplaires que vous désirez. Je crois que les avantages symboliques et moraux de mon projet sont tels qu'il faudrait faire tous les efforts pour aboutir à son adoption, y compris l'élimination des défauts qu'ils puissent présenter sous sa forme actuelle.

    Permettez-moi tout d'abord de relever le reproche que vous lui faites: qu'il ne saurait être reproduit par des particuliers. Je ne crois pas vraiment qu'il soit de nature à nous arrêter. Le drapeau britannique en est là, et plusieurs autres; et je crois, du reste, que la popularité doit venir comme l'ultime conséquence d'une campagne commencée par en haut.

    Je crois que l'or pour les étoiles a le défaut de disparaître sous certains angles; et, quoique l'or permettrait de très beaux effets dans certains cas, par exemple des étoiles brodées sur soie bleue, il serait peut-être plus pratique parce que plus visible, de faire les étoiles jaunes pour les drapeaux courants. On pourrait aussi les faire un peu plus grandes.

    Vous pourriez peut-être transmettre à qui de droit ces aménagements que je suggère moi-même; ainsi que mes regrets de l'omission du Luxembourg. Mais j'insiste encore sur le fait que c'est le seul drapeau qui correspond exactement à l'Europe, à son unité et aussi à toute ses nations.

    Je vous serais obligé de me tenir au courant du développement de la question et en attendant je vous envoie mes sentiments les plus cordiaux.

I
PL/SD

Cher Monsieur Martin,

A la suite de notre récente conversation, j'ai le plaisir de vous envoyer, sous ce pli, les modèles de drapeaux qui ont été soumis récemment aux Représentants à l'Assemblée Consultative. J'y ai ajouté la proposition qui vient d'être faite par Monsieur Salvador de Madariaga.

Sur 48 réponses reçues des membres de l'Assemblée, 23 mettent au premier rang le N° 1, 9 mettent en premier rang le N° 7 et aucune ne mettent en premier rang le N° 4 qui vous intéresse particulièrement. Les deux membres de l'Assemblée qui citent cependant le 4 parmi les solutions possibles demandent qu'on supprime le blason.

Il y a enfin une objection générale des Turcs et d'un Britannique contre tout emblème portant la croix.

J'en profite pour annexer à ce pli le catalogue du Musée du Caillou.

Veuillez, je vous prie, transmettre mes hommages à Madame Martin et lui dire combien nous avons été heureux de pouvoir passer quelques heures avec vous.

Croyez-moi, cher Monsieur Martin, votre tout dévoué,

Paul M.G. LEVY
Directeur de l'Information

Monsieur Paul Martin
Conservateur des Musées de Strasbourg.
Palais de Rohan. STRASBOURG

CONSEIL DE L'EUROPE

SECRÉTARIAT GÉNÉRAL

Prière d'adresser le courrier officiel:
SECRÉTAIRE GÉNÉRAL, ou bien SECRÉTARIAT GÉNÉRAL
Please address official correspondance to the:
SECRETARY-GENERAL, or SECRETARIAT-GENERAL

Adresse télégraphique: EUROPA Strasbourg
Telegraphic address: EUROPA Strasbourg
Téléphone 534.00 à 09

COUNCIL OF EUROPE

SECRETARIAT-GENERAL

No A. 1410

15th February 1952

Sir,

Emblem of the Council of Europe

At the request of the Committee on Rules of Procedure and Privileges a referendum was held among all Representatives during the last few days of the Third Session of the Assembly on various proposals put forward for an emblem of the Council of Europe.

The results of this referendum are as follows:

48 Representatives have so far returned the questionnaire submitted to them.

Of these 48 Representatives, 2 rejected all the proposals submitted, 16 favoured one only and 14 placed the twelve proposals in order of preference as requested.

23 of the 48 replies - that is, nearly half - gave first preference to Proposal No.1: the flag of Count Coudenhove, on a field azure a gold sun bearing a cross gules. This proposal also came second twice, third twice, fifth once, sixth once, tenth once and eleventh once.

Among the comments and suggestions made about this proposal, the following should be noted:

a) No emblem of an institution of which Moslems are members may bear a cross. (Comment of a Turkish and a British Representative).

b) The general design could be retained with the addition of a crescent in the upper left-hand quarter when the emblem is used in Moslem countries;

c) Both the sun and the cross should be placed in the upper left-hand quarter;

d) The cross might extend to the edges of the flag in both directions.

A.7642
TG.726/VT/NB.

./.

The proposal obtaining the second largest number of votes was No.7 (the reverse of the American flag). It came first 9 times, second 6 times, third twice, fourth once, fifth once, seventh 3 times, eighth, ninth and tenth once each.

Among the comments on this proposal the following may be noted:

a) It is too American;

b) It is good because it is American;

c) The barry should consist of 10 pieces instead of 13.

Other proposals given first preference were as follows:

No. 2 5 times.
No. 3 twice.
No. 5 once.
No. 9 once.
No.10 twice.
No.11 once.
No.12 twice.

Among the general comments accompanying the replies the following are worthy of note:

a) Green is not a good colour since it quickly fades;

b) Only the Coudenhove proposal is possible;

c) Only Proposals 2 and 3 (cross argent on a field vert and a cross gules on a field argent) are possible;

d) Proposal No 4 might be adopted but without the Strasbourg coat-of-arms in the centre;

e) Proposal No 11 (on a field gules a sun or, and "Europa" in gold lettering) might be adopted without the white hand (two identical replies);

f) The idea of a flag with stars only, like No.12, might be adopted but in different colours (on a field gules stars argent). This, however, is too servilely American, state two Representatives.

A.7642

g) 4 Representatives asked for a further investigation
    into the whole problem.

I thought you would like to know the results of this
inquiry which will be submitted to the Committee on Rules of
Procedure and Privileges at its next meeting.

I am, Sir,
Your obedient Servant,

F. CARACCIOLO.
Deputy Secretary-General
Clerk of the Assembly

A.7642

I
PL/SD

Cher Monsieur de Madariaga,

Je vous remercie de m'avoir envoyé 250 copies de votre projet de drapeau. Je les ferai tenir aux Représentants dans le plus prochain pli que je leur enverrai. J'y ajouterai une note reprenant les quelques observations que vous faites vous-même.

Je m'en voudrais de discuter plus avant le problème en attendant de connaître les réponses des membres de l'Assemblée. Il est évident cependant que le précédent du drapeau britannique que vous invoquez est parfaitement exact. On pourrait ajouter que la situation n'est pas tout-à-fait comparable .....

Je ne manquerai pas de vous tenir au courant des réactions éventuelles. Il est certain que devant les résultats du premier sondage auquel nous avons procédé, une proposition entièrement nouvelle comme la vôtre ne manque pas d'intérêt. Dans l'ensemble ledit sondage auquel ont réagi 48 membres de l'Assemblée a donné 23 fois la préférence à l'emblème du Comte Coudenhove, et 9 fois au négatif du drapeau américain .... avec cependant quelques objections venant notamment de son apparence trop américaine. D'autre part, les Turcs nous ont fait savoir qu'ils ne pourraient se rallier en aucun cas à un drapeau portant la croix, ce qui du même coup élimine le projet Coudenhove.

Croyez-moi, cher Monsieur de Madariaga, votre très cordialement dévoué,

Paul M.G. LEVY
Directeur de l'Information

Mr Salvador de Madariaga
3, Church Street,
Old Headington
OXFORD

2191
2868
2 7 MARS 1952
(203)

I
PL/SD

Mon cher Comte,

Plus de trois mois s'étant écoulés depuis la date limite
pour l'envoi des réponses à notre sondage d'opinion sur le
drapeau, nous avons considéré que cette enquête était terminée.
Toute nouvelle réponse qui nous parviendrait ne serait donc
pas considérée comme faisant partie de cette enquête.

Je ne vous cache pas que la chose qui me préoccupe le
plus depuis la fin de ladite enquête, c'est que, si une majorité très nette (encore que relative) s'est dégagée en faveur
de votre projet, la seule objection de principe qui ait été
formulée est celle des Turcs, dirigée contre l'utilisation
de la croix.
Je le regrette d'autant plus que, comme vous le savez,
j'étais moi-même très favorable à la présence d'une croix
dans le drapeau et je m'étais laissé dire qu'aucune objection
ne serait soulevée du côté musulman. Il en va autrement, et
je le regrette beaucoup.
Voyez-vous une solution de votre côté ?

Croyez-moi, mon cher Comte, votre bien sincèrement dévoué,

Paul M.G. LEVY
Directeur de l'Information

Comte Coudenhove-Kalergi
Hôtel "Raphaël"

17, Avenue Kléber
PARIS.

VO4.136.3   2191

MOUVEMENT 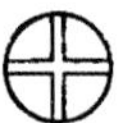 PANEUROPÉEN

POUR LES ÉTATS-UNIS D'EUROPE
FONDÉ EN 1923

(204)

Président :
R. COUDENHOVE-KALERGI

GSTAAD (SUISSE)

Paris, le 15 avril 1952.

Mon cher Ami,

  Je vous remercie de votre lettre du 27 mars dernier concernant le drapeau de l'Europe.

  Je crois que l'objection musulmane peut être surmontés si on ajoute au drapeau de la croix sur le soleil un petit croissant dans le coin.

  Comme le bleu symbolise le ciel, il y a la place pour les deux, le soleil et la lune.

  Je pense que si cette solution est acceptée par les Turcs, l'unanimité sur ce drapeau pourrait être assurée.

  Croyez, Cher Ami, à mes sentiments sincèrement dévoués.

Richard Coudenhove-Kalergi

Monsieur G. LEVY
Directeur de l'Information
CONSEIL de l'EUROPE
STRASBOURG

4634

12 MAI 1952

I
PL/BD

Mon cher Comte,

J'ai accordé la plus grande attention à
l'intéressante suggestion que vous m'avez faite.dansovotre
lettre du 15 avril. Je pense qu'elle permettrait en effet
d'écarter les objections faites par les Représentants turcs.
Vous concevrez pourtant qu'il m'est très délicat, comme
fonctionnaire du Conseil de l'Europe, d'intervenir dans ce
sens.

Je suggèrerai donc que vous preniez l'initiative,
et cela de deux façons :
a) en touchant vous-même vos amis turcs et en préparant
le terrain parmi eux; éventuellement en suggérant qu'ils fas-
sent eux-mêmes la proposition en donnant leur accord pour que
la croix rouge sur le soleil d'or soit utilisée moyennant
version spéciale pour usage en Turquie portant un croissant
supplémentaire;
b) en préparant le terrain du côté des autres Représentants
et en vous assurant d'un appui suffisant parmi eux.
Je vous rappelle que le membre turc de la Commission du Règlement devant laquelle le problème est posé en ce
moment est Monsieur MANDALINCI, la Commission a pour Président
Monsieur Van Cauwelaert, vice-présidents : MM. Benvenuti
et Hoy (si je suis bien informé, ce dernier ne viendrait
plus à Strasbourg). Vous trouverez la composition de la
Commission à la page 103 de l'Annuaire de l'Assemblée.

Ladite Commission doit se réunir à Strasbourg,
le samedi 24 mai à 10 heures.

Veuillez, je vous prie, transmettre mes hommages
à la Comtesse, et recevoir l'assurance de mon souvenir très
dévoué,

                                        Paul M.G. LEVY
Cte Coudenhove-Kalergi   Directeur de l'Information

211

Richard Comte de Coudenhove-Kalergi

mom.à Baden-Baden,Brenner's
Parkhotel,
le 17-5-52

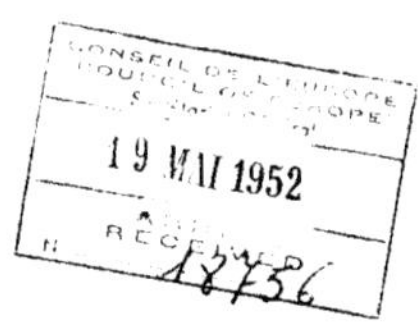

Monsieur Paul M.G.LEVY
Directeur de l'Information
Conseil de l'Europe,

Cher ami,
Vous trouverez ci-joint la copie que je viens d'adres=
ser à Monsieur Cauwelaert et dont j'ai donné copie aux Mes=
sieurs Benvenuti et Mandalinci. J'espère que la question
pourra être réglée de cette façon.

Dans ma pensée le drapeau de l'Armée Européenne, qui
ne contient que des états chrétiens, devrait être sans crois=
sant, tandis que le drapeau des Conseils de l'Europe devrait
y ajouter un croissant.

Veuillez, je vous prie, transmettre mes hommages à Ma=
dame Levy, et croyez, cher ami, à mes sentiments très dé=
voués,

Richard Coudenhove-Kalergi

Annexe

Richard Comte de Coudenhove-Kalergi

mom.à Baden-Baden, Brenner's Parkhotel,
le 17-5-52

S.Exc.
Monsieur le Ministre van Cauwelaert
Président de la Chambre des Représentants

B r u x e l l e s .
==============================

Mon cher Président et Ami,

Comme vous savez, l'enquête sur le drapeau européen, or=
ganisée par le Conseil de l'Europe, a donné une forte majo=
rité relative au drapeau de la croix rouge sur un soleil d'or
sur le fond bleu.

La seule difficulté qui se pose c'est l'opposition des
turcs contre le symbole de la croix. Afin de le faire accep=
table aux turcs, je proposerais de placer le croissant au
coin gauche du drapeau. Je crois que par ce moyen l'opposi=
tion turque pourrait être surmontée et l'unanimité, ou bien
la grande majorité, gàrantie au plus beau et plus ancien
symbole européen.

Croyez, mon cher Président et Ami, à mes sentiments
sincères et dévoués,

213

Ambassade de Turquie

Paris, le 16 Juin 1952

17 JUIN 1952
RECEIVED

Mon cher Directeur,

Me référant à la demande que vous aviez faite
à M. Ebuzzia, député turc représentant à l'Assemblée
Consultative, je vous fais parvenir, sous ce pli, un
schéma montrant les proportions exactes des dimensions
du drapeau turc.

Veuillez agréer, mon cher Directeur, les
assurances de ma considération distinguée.

C. S. Hayta

Conseiller de l'Ambassade

Monsieur Lévy
Directeur de l'Information
du Conseil de l'Europe

S t r a s b o u r g

I
PL/SD

Mon cher Comte,

      Je ne vous ai rien fait savoir au sujet de récents développements concernant le drapeau européen pour cette simple raison que l'Assemblée ne s'en est pas occupée au cours de sa dernière session.

      La Commission du Règlement qui avait la chose à son ordre du jour, n'a pas cru pouvoir aberder le sujet.

      J'ai eu cependant plusieurs conversations sur ce point avec des membres de l'Assemblée et diverses personnalités. Je vous envoie ci-joint le texte d'une note que je viens de rédiger à l'intention de M. le Président van Cauwelaert. J'aimerais beaucoup avoir votre avis sur son contenu.

      J'envoie également une documentation à M. le Ministre Bech ; je comprends qu'il n'ait jamais vu les projets, puisque l'affaire n'est jamais arrivée au stade du Comité des Ministres.

      Soyez assez aimable pour transmettre mes hommages respectueux à la Comtesse, et recevez, mon cher Comte, l'expression de mes sentiments les plus dévoués.

              Paul M.G. LEVY
           Directeur de l'Information

Comte Coudenhove-Kalergi
Brenner's Parkhotel
Baden-Baden

5806
214
JUIN 1952
215

I
PL/SD

Mon cher Conseiller,

Je vous remercie beaucoup pour
les précieuses indications que vous m'avez envoyées au
sujet du drapeau turc.

Puis-je saisir cette occasion
pour vous signaler que le 14 mars de cette année j'avais
demandé aux divers départements des Affaires Etrangères de
bien vouloir me donner la description officielle du drapeau
national, ainsi que des indications très complètes au sujet
de l'origine et de l'histoire du drapeau, avec des références
aux textes officiels éventuels fixant la forme de l'emblème.

Je suis maintenant, grâce à votre
grande obligeance, en possession de la description officielle
du drapeau turc. Pourrais-je vous mettre encore à contribution en vous demandant s'il serait possible que vous me
fournissiez les autres renseignements : histoire, et textes
légaux de référence.

Je vous en remercie d'avance, et
vous prie de croire, mon cher Conseiller, à mes sentiments
dévoués et très distingués.

Paul M.G. LEVY
Directeur de l'Information

Monsieur C.S. Hayta
Conseiller de l'Ambassade de Turquie
délégué du Ministre des Affaires
Etrangères de Turquie
PARIS.

JUIN 1952

2191

216

I

PL/SD

Monsieur le Président,

Je me permets de vous envoyer sous ce pli une note que je viens de rédiger à votre intention, sur l'état du problème de l'emblème européen.

Je vous serais infiniment reconnaissant si vous pouviez me faire connaître votre avis et notamment me faire savoir si vous croyez utile que je poursuive l'examen de la question dans ce sens, en vue de la prochaine réunion de la Commission du Règlement.

Veuillez agréer, Monsieur le Président, l'assurance de ma très haute considération.

Paul M. G. LEVY
Directeur de l'Information

Monsieur van Cauwelaert
Président de la Commission
du Règlement et des Prérogatives
de l'Assemblée Consultative du
Conseil de l'Europe.

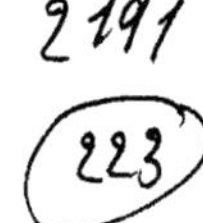

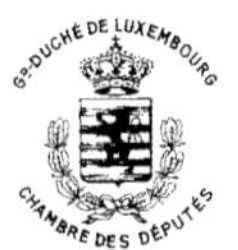

X07.136.3

2191

(223)

Luxembourg, le 18 juillet 1952.

Au Secrétariat général
du Conseil de l'Europe,
à l'attention de Monsieur
M.G. LEVY,
Directeur des Services d'Information
du Conseil de l'Europe,
à   S t r a s b o u r g,
Place Lenôtre.

Monsieur le Directeur,

J'ai l'honneur de vous prier de bien vouloir me faire parvenir 3 exemplaires de votre étude " Un drapeau pour l'Europe " (Extrait de Saisons d'Alsace N° 3 - 1950).

En vous remerciant, je vous présente, Monsieur le Directeur, l'assurance de ma haute considération.

Le Secrétaire général de la Chambre des Députés,

(Marcel MERIS, docteur en droit.)

X.IV.136.3
2191
7737
924
1 8 AOUT 1952

I

PL/ND

Monsieur le Secrétaire Général,

A mon retour de vacances je prends
connaissance de votre lettre du 18 juillet à laquelle mes
collaborateurs n'avaient pas répondu parce qu'ils pensaient
que nous ne possédions plus d'exemplaire de l'article qui
vous intéresse.

J'ai pu mettre la main sur 1 exemplaire
qui restait chez moi et que je ne voulais pas distribuer,
le drapeau de la République Fédérale d'Allemagne étant mal
représenté. Je vous prie donc de considérer la feuille
intercalaire comme un rectificatif.

Je dois ajouter que depuis que j'ai
fait cette étude, la situation a évolué et que l'opposition
des Turcs à la présence d'une croix sur le drapeau m'oblige
en ce moment à considérer une proposition entièrement
nouvelle que je compte soumettre à la prochaine réunion de
la Commission du Règlement de l'Assemblée Consultative.

Veuillez croire, Monsieur le Secrétaire
Général, à mes sentiments les plus distingués.

                          Paul M.G. LEVY
                       Directeur de l'Information

Monsieur Marcel Meris
Secrétaire Général de la
Chambre des Députés
LUXEMBOURG.

KO7.156.3
9191.
1071. (257)

I

PL/BD

1 OCT. 1953

Monsieur le Président,

Je vous remercie pour votre aimable note du
14 septembre me faisant connaître les propositions adoptées par
le Comité militaire du Comité Intérimaire de la Communauté
Européenne de Défense en date du 5 mars 1953.

Je ne sais si je me trompe, mais j'ai l'impres-
sion que les auteurs de cette proposition sont partis de l'idée
que l'insigne du E vert sur fond blanc, utilisé par le Mouvement
Européen, était déjà adopté en principe comme pavillon officiel
de l'Europe unie.

L'Assemblée Consultative du Conseil de l'Europe
qui, depuis 1950, se préoccupait du problème d'un emblème européen a pris une première décision au cours de sa dernière session.
Afin de mettre un terme à l'incertitude et, estimant qu'elle
devait en agissant dans le cadre de sa compétence propre, poser
un acte ayant une valeur définitive, elle a adopté pour emblème
le drapeau dont vous trouverez le modèle ci-joint. Ce vote a
été acquis le 25 septembre par 49 voix contre 17 et 7 abstentions.

Quelques instants plus tard, par 54 voix contre
17 et 7 abstentions, l'Assemblée recommandait au Comité des Ministres du Conseil de l'Europe d'adopter cet emblème pour l'ensemble du Conseil et de charger le Secrétaire Général d'entrer
en rapport avec les autres institutions européennes pour que
ces dernières adoptent des emblèmes apparentés au sien.

Je me permets d'attirer votre attention sur deux
points particuliers :

— L'Assemblée n'a pas voulu dépasser les limites
de sa compétence. Elle ne pouvait donc ni adopter seule un

./.

- 2 -

emblème du Conseil de l'Europe, ni adopter seule un emblème
de l'Europe. Mais elle tenait à être le premier organisme
européen à prendre une décision officielle dans cette voie.
Son désir est évidemment que son emblème connaisse le plus
large usage.

          - La presse a donné différents commentaires au
sujet des votes négatifs et des abstentions émis à l'occasion du
choix d'un emblème. Je crois pouvoir assurer que, contrairement
à ce qu'ont écrit certains journaux, dans aucun cas les députés
n'ont voulu défendre le E vert sur fond blanc qui, depuis des
années, est l'objet de leur critique. Les seules questions qui
se soient posées pour eux sont d'une part celle de l'opportunité
de l'existence d'un symbole européen (les abstentions) et de la
présence, dans cet emblème, d'une quinzième étoile représentant
la Sarre. C'est pour cette dernière raison que la plupart des
Représentants allemands ont voté contre. Mais cette même question a été résolue quelques instants plus tard à l'intervention
du député allemand M. [illegible] qui a proposé que, dans la description du drapeau, on dise que les étoiles représentent les
quinze "Membres du Conseil de l'Europe" et non point quinze
"Nations". Cette modification a été aussitôt apportée aux
documents et la question paraît dès lors être résolue.

          Je vous envoie en annexe le rapport présenté
par M. Bichet à l'Assemblée Consultative au nom de la Commission
du Règlement et des Prérogatives, le document descriptif du
drapeau amendé sur la suggestion de l'Assemblée, et les textes
officiels de la résolution et de la recommandation adoptées.

          Je vous prie de croire, Monsieur le Président,
à mes sentiments les plus distingués.

                    Paul M.G. LEVY
                 Directeur de l'Information

Monsieur Roger Gromand
Président du
Comité de l'Information
Comité Intérimaire de la Conférence
pour l'Organisation de la Communauté
Européenne de Défense.
Ministère des Affaires Etrangères.
PARIS.

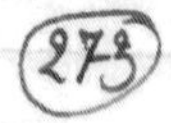

HISTORIQUE DE LA QUESTION DE L'EMBLÈME

I. Dès la constitution du Conseil de l'Europe de nombreux correspondants se sont enquis de la forme de l'emblème du Conseil. Parfois les emblèmes de mouvements privés ont été pris pour un symbole officiel. Certaines propositions aussi ont été faite spontanément.

2. La question a été portée à la connaissance du Bureau de l'Assemblée par le Secrétaire Général à la fin de 1949. Le Bureau a estimé alors que l'Assemblée dans son ensemble devrait se prononcer et qu'une sous-commission devrait éventuellement être constituée pour préparer un rapport sur la question.

3. Au début de 1950, l'Union Parlementaire Européenne a proposé au Secrétaire Général l'adoption de l'emblème du Mouvement paneuropéen.

4. Le 23 Juin 1950, la Commission des Affaires Générale demanda au Secrétaire Général d'établir un rapport sur les dispositions susceptibles d'être prises en vue de rendre directement sensibles à l'opinion publique la réalité de l'union européenne. Ce rapport fut préparé et présenté à l'Assemblée sous la forme de l'annexe II du document AS (2) 85.

4. Le 18 août 1950, l'Assemblée Consultative confirma cette résolution de la Commission des Affaires Générales et le 28 août elle demanda à chacune de ses commissions compétentes d'examiner les suggestions contenues dans le document du Secrétariat Général. La première des propositions se rapportait au " drapeau européen " et fut renvoyée à la Commission du Règlement et des Prérogatives.

6. (Dans l'entretemps, l'Assemblée Nationale française était saisie d'une proposition de M. Bichet, représentant à l'Assemblée Consultative demandant que l'emblème du Mouvement Européen soit arboré sur les édifices publics français : des campagnes se développaient pour l'emploi de l'emblème du Mouvement Européen et la confusion s'étendait.)

7. Le 26 juillet 1951, la Sous-Commission des Immunités de la Commission du Règlement et des Prérogatives examinait le rapport établi par le Secrétariat Général (AS/RPP II (3) 2) et décidait que :
    a) en principe, il est désirable que le Conseil de l'Europe soit doté de son drapeau et emblème propres ;
    b) le Secrétariat Général est invité à préparer un mémorandum résumant les suggestions faites pour l'emblème, les règles à adopter pour son emploi et les mesures législatives nécessaires pour lui assurer le respect généralement accordé aux drapeaux nationaux.

8. Le 27 novembre 1951, la réunion plénière de la Commission du Règlement et des Prérogatives se saisit de la question et décide

de sonder l'opinion des Représentants avant d'examiner elle-même
la forme de l'emblème.

9. Suivant les instructions de la Commission, une enquête est
faite parmi les membres de l'Assemblée. Les résultats en sont commu-
niqués par lettre du Greffier en date du 13 février 1952. Quarante
huit représentants ont répondu dont 23 se sont prononcés en faveur
de l'emblème du mouvement paneuropéen. Cependant il comporte une
Croix et des oppositions de principe se sont manifestées.

10. Don Salvador de Madariaga, Président du Centre Européen de la
Culture propose un drapeau bleu étoilé d'or et demande qu'il soit
soumis à l'Assemblée

11. Le 30 août 1952 l'Europa-Union de Hambourg à la suite d'un
concours public retient plusieurs projets dont le drapeau bleu à
cercles d'étoiles d'or.

12. La Commission du Règlement et des Prérogatives demande un nouveau rapport au Secrétariat Général. Retenu par d'autres sujets de
travail elle en remet plusieurs fois l'examen en question. Finalement le rapport lui est présenté en mai 1953 (AS/RPP (5) 1). La
Commission, réunie le 20 mai retient en principe et à titre de
simple projet le drapeau à champ d'azur cercle d'étoiles d'or. Elle
décide de faire consulter officieusement la Haute Autorité de la
C.E.C.A. et la Commission Intérimaire de la C.E.D. M. Bichet est dé-
signé comme rapporteur.

13. La consultation officieuse demandée par la Commission a lieu.
La Haute Autorité de la C.E.C.A. est en principe décidée à ne pas
avoir d'emblème tant que n'existera pas la Communauté Politique ;
à ce moment elle adoptera le drapeau " fédéral ". Quant à la C.E.D
son Comité militaire a déjà adopté secrètement le drapeau blanc
portant le E vert du Mouvement Européen, découpé en triple flamme.

14. Le 17 septembre 1953, M. Bichet présente son rapport à la Commission : Tout en n'abandonnant pas le premier projet retenu par la
Commission, il déclare préférable de revenir au blanc et au vert.
Il propose un projet de Recommandation qui comporte l'adoption de
l'emblème par l'Assemblée et la recommandation au Comité des Ministres
d'inviter les Membres à adopter cet emblème commun. La Commission
décide de maintenant les couleurs bleu et or auxquelles elle s'était
ralliée en mai et charge M. Bichet d'établir le texte définitif de
son rapport.

15. Le 18 septembre 1953, l'Assemblée décide d'inscrire la question
à son ordre du jour.

16. Le 21 décembre, M. Bichet dépose son rapport (document 198 de
la cinquième session ordinaire) qui contient un projet de Résolution
et un projet de Recommandation. Il indique que cette procédure est
suggérée parce qu'il a paru " périlleux de faire passer cet emblème

par une procédure longue et laborieuse avant de pouvoir en faire un emploi effectif ". En effet; c'est la crainte de voir d'autres institutions adopter des emblèmes n'ayant aucune parenté avec celui du Conseil qui conduit la Commission à brusquer les choses : cette préoccupation apparaît nettement dans le § (b) du projet de Recommandation. Quant à la description de l'emblème, le rapporteur a évité de parler des " membres du Conseil de l'Europe et a préféré le terme "nations représentées à l'Assemblée Consultative."

17. Le 25 septembre la question vint en séance plénière. Après l'exposé de M.Bichet, M.Erler attirant l'attention de l'Assemblée sur les difficultés que la proposition pourrait rencontrer au Comité des Ministres, demanda le renvoi à la Commission des Affaires générales pour avis. Cette proposition fut combattue par M.Braun et par le rapporteur qui souligna que, quelle que soit la décision de l'Assemblée, la décision finale restait au Comité des Ministres qui aurait " a apprécier, à interpréter et à décider " et " qui est le mieux qualifié pour juger de l'aspect politique des décisions à prendre ". La proposition de renvoi en Commission fut rejetée. La Résolution fut adoptée par 49 voix contre 17 et 6 abstentions et la Recommandation par 54 voix contre 17 et 7 abstentions.

18. A la demande de M. Kiesinger, la description symbolique de l'emblème fut amendée et le mot "Membre " fut substitué à celui de " Nations ".

19. Le 16 janvier, à la réunion du Bureau de l'Assemblée, le Président a annoncé que le gouvernement allemand ayant soulevé certaines objections ,le Bureau devrait examiner la question dès que le Comité des Ministres l'en saisirait.

2191.
(274)

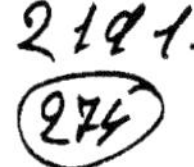

NOTE SUR L'ADOPTION DEFINITIVE DU DRAPEAU ACCEPTE PAR L'ASSEMBLEE CONSULTATIVE

1.RAISONS **D'ACCELERER LA PROCEDURE**-On a beaucoup trop tardé à se prononcer officiellement sur un emblème européen.Le E vert sur fond blanc s'est de plus en plus imposé tout en étant de plus en plus honni. Pour mettre un terme à l'incertitude et aux flottements,l'Assemblée Consultative a adopté définitivement pour son emblème le pavillon bleu à cercle de quinze étoiles d'or.

2.LE PROBLEME DE LA QUINZIEME ETOILE-Le 25/9/53 lors de la discussion à l'Assemblée Consultative,un député socialiste allemand a cru pouvoir interpréter la présence de quinze étoiles sur le drapeau comme une reconnaissance du caractère définitif d'un statut autonome de la Sarre.Ceci a provoqué une discussion qu'il a été impossible de mener à fond présisément pour ne pas compromettre le débat sur la Sarre qui allait s'ouvrir.Devant les questions soulevées,certains députés ont voté contre ou se sont abstenus,généralement pour éviter de choquer ceux qui avaient pris l'une ou l'autre position sur le fond du débat.

Après le vote,un député C.D.U. allemand a demandé que la description symbolique du drapeau se trouvant xxxxxxxxxx dans le document annexé au rapport de la Commission du Règlement et des Prérogatives dise que les étoiles représentent "les Membres du Conseil de l'Europe" et non point les "nations représentées à l'Assemblée Consultative". Or le mot nation avait été pris dans son sens le plus général et le chiffre de quinze ne lui était nulle part associé. Les nations européennes (ou les peuples européens) forment le cercle en signe d'union.L'ensemble de ces nations est représenté par un cercle de 15 étoiles.

point parce qu'il y a quinze nations(ce nombr e est plus grand ou plus petit suivant la conc eption qu'on a de la nation)mais parce qu'au moment de l'adoption de l'emblème il y avait au Conseil de l'Europe quinze Membr représentant les nations libres d'Europe.

Il faut ajouter d'ailleurs que la Résolution et la Recommandation de l'Assemblée Consultative décrive l'emblème comme étant d'azur à cercle de quinze étoiles d'or et non point comme d'azur à cercle d'étoiles d'or en nombre égal à celui des Membres du Conseil de l'Europe ce quix signifie bien que le nombre 15 a été adopté une fois pour toutes et ne sera pas soumis à révision qu'il y ait augmentation ou diminution du nombre des Membres.

Ceci souligne le fait que le problème du pavillon n'est aucunement lié à celui de la Sarre.Il faut donc accélérer son adoption définitive et non point la retarder.

Nous ajouterons que la première proposition d'un cercle de quinze étoiles d'or sur fond bleu a été formulée en septembre 1951 par la section de Hambourg de l'Europa-Union qui en réclame aujourd'hui la paternité.En réalité des recherches parallèles ont conduit la même solution qui paraît la plus harmonieuse au point de vue esthétique,qui ne souffre pas de critique au point de vue héraldique et à laquelle il serait contre-indiqué d'apporter des modifications dans l'avenir.

Si MM.Bidault et Adenauer pouvaient se mettre d'accord pour présenter le projet au Comité des Ministres(ou plutôt pour l'appuyer) il n'y aurait aucune objection de la part des autres gouvernements.

V04,136,3

DER STAATSSEKRETÄR
DES AUSWÄRTIGEN AMTS   BONN,   December 1953.

221-53 II 15802/53

        Sir,

                With reference to Resolution 41 of the Consultative
        Assembly of 25th September regarding the choice of an
        emblem for the Assembly, and to Recommendation 56 of the
        Consultative Assembly of the same date with regard to the
        adoption of this emblem for the Council of Europe as a
        whole, I beg to draw attention to the following points :

                The choice of an emblem for any one organ of the
        Council of Europe such as the Consultative Assembly, is a
        matter that concerns the Council as a whole. It would,
        in any case, appear that the Assembly shares this view
        since in Recommendation 56, it specifically recommends the
        adoption of this emblem by the entire Council.

                In view of the importance to be attributed to an
        emblem of any kind which is the symbol of a political
        organ, such a matter should be settled in an orderly
        fashion. Under Articles 13 and 16 of the Statute of the
        Council of Europe, the Committee of Ministers is the organ
        competent to consider and propose any action required to
        further the aim of the Council of Europe. This applies
        more particularly to any matter of a specifically political
        character, which is certainly the case where the choice of
        an emblem for a part or the whole of the Council of Europe
        is concerned. The choice of such an emblem is, at any rate,
        a matter relating to the internal organisation and arrange-
        ments of the Council of Europe, and this, under Article 16,
        para. 1 of the Statute, falls within the sole competence
        of the Committee of Ministers. The relevant decisions of
        the Consultative Assembly therefore encroach upon the
        statutory powers of the Committee of Ministers.

M. Léon MARCHAL
Secretary-General,   ./.
Council of Europe,

STRASBOURG

15.462

The Federal Government thus considers that the adoption
of a special emblem for the Consultative Assembly is open
to certain objections, particularly in view of the fact that
the Member Governments of the Council of Europe have not so
far consulted each other as to whether the adoption of an
emblem for the Council of Europe would not demand a prior
addition to its Statute.

Only after some light has been shed on this matter
can the question of the form this emblem should assume be
submitted to the Committee of Ministers for discussion.

I am, Sir,
Your obedient Servant,

(signed: HALLSTEIN)

ASSEMBLÉE PARLEMENTAIRE
EUROPÉENNE

LE PRÉSIDENT
127, rue de Grenelle
PARIS-7e

Paris, le 12 février 1959

HB/MV

Monsieur le Directeur,

Votre lettre PL/CS, non datée, vient de me parvenir.

A titre personnel, je me rallie au choix de l'emblème européen officiel "cercle de 12 étoiles d'or sur champ d'azur".

Cordialement votre,

Robert SCHUMAN

Monsieur Paul M.G. LEVY
Directeur de l'Information
du Conseil de l'Europe
STRASBOURG

Biographies

Remco Torenbosch (1982) lives and
work in the Netherlands. In his work he
investigates social-economic changes
in (recent) world history. Torenbosch
participated in group exhibitions and public
events at Kunsthalle Wien (2014), MMKA,
Arnhem (2014), de Appel, Amsterdam (2013),
San Serriffe, Amsterdam (2013), GAMeC,
Bergamo (2012), Temporary Gallery, Cologne
(2012), De Vleeshal, Middelburg (2012),
Stroom, The Hague (2011), Casco in collaboration with W139, Amsterdam (2011),
Kunstraum, Innsbruck (2009).

Charles Esche (1962) is a curator, writer
and the director of Van Abbemuseum,
Eindhoven. Esche has (co-)curated
biennials in São Paulo (2014), Ljubljana
(2010), Brussels (2008), Ramallah (2007),
Istanbul (2005) and Gwangju (2002). He
has written for numerous catalogues and
magazines and published an edited volume
of his writings in Turkish and English,
Modest Proposals (Istanbul: Baglam
Publishing, 2005). A Senior Research Fellow
at Central Saint Martins College of Art
and Design, Esche is the co-founder and
Editorial Director of Afterall Books, and an
Editor for the *Exhibition Histories* book
series. He co-edited (with Will Bradley) Art
and *Social Change* (London: Tate Publishing
in association with Afterall, 2007). In 2012
he received the European Cultural
Foundation's Princess Margriet Award.

Mihnea Mircan (1976) is a curator, writer and
the artistic director of Extra City Kunsthal,
Antwerp. Mihnea curated exhibitions
such as: Sean Snyder (with Florin Tudor)
(2007), SUBLIME OBJECTS (2007), Video
Works—Jaan Toomik (2005), and the
series of site-specific interventions *Under
Destruction* (2004–2007). His other curatorial
projects include: Image to be projected until
it vanishes, Museion, Bolzano (2011), History
of Art, the, David Roberts Art Foundation,
London (2010), and Low-Budget Monuments,
Romanian Pavilion, 52nd Venice Biennale,
Venice (2007).

The Council of Europe (1949) is the
continent's leading human rights
organisation. It includes 47 member states,
28 of which are members of the European
Union. All Council of Europe member states
have signed up to the European Convention
on Human Rights, a treaty designed to
protect human rights, democracy and the
rule of law. The European Court of Human
Rights oversees the implementation of
the Convention in the member states.
Individuals can bring complaints of human
rights violations to the Strasbourg Court
once all possibilities of appeal have been
exhausted in the member state concerned.
The European Union is preparing to sign
the European Convention on Human Rights,
creating a common European legal space
for over 820 million citizens. The Council of
Europe has its headquarters in Strasbourg,
France. It employs 2 200 people, and
maintains external and liaison offices to
other international organisations. The
European Youth Centres in Strasbourg and
Budapest offer training for young people in
democracy and human rights issues.

The European Foundation for the
Improvement of Living and Working
Conditions (1975) is a tripartite European
Union Agency, whose role is to provide
knowledge in the area of social and work-
related policies.

Eurofound was established in 1975 by
Council Regulation (EEC) No. 1365/75
to contribute to the planning and design
of better living and working conditions
in Europe.

The European Monitoring Centre on
Change (2001) is an information resource
established to promote an understanding
of changes in the world of work, employment
and restructuring. It was set up in 2001
within the European Foundation for the
Improvement of Living and Working
Conditions, Dublin, with the full support
of the European Parliament, the European
Commission and the social partners.

Acknowledgements

Austria
Nicole van der Pauw
assistant economic department
Embassy of the Kingdom of
the Netherlands Vienna

Ursula Feyerer
labour and social law
Association of the textile, clothing,
and leather industry

Birgit Nemec
officer
Österreichische Textil Zeitung

Belgium
Jacqueline van Noordenne
press, politics and culture
Embassy of the Kingdom of
the Netherlands Brussels

Tim Lohmann
economic department
Embassy of the Kingdom of the
Netherlands Brussels

Bulgaria
Janette Verrijzer
economic department
Embassy of the Kingdom of
the Netherlands Sofia

Deliana Petrova
international projects
Bulgarian association of Apparel
and Textile Producers

Croatia
Nataša Galo Samac
Embassy of the Kingdom of
the Netherlands Zagreb

Andreja Kocijan
Embassy of the Kingdom of
the Netherlands Zagreb

Zrinka Paladino
deputy head of office
Zagreb City Office for
Monumental Protection

Svjetlana Sokcevic
officer
Croatian branch related
textile trade union

Goran Arcabic
curator
Zagreb City Museum

Cyprus
Ingrid Christodoulou
economic affairs
Embassy of the Kingdom of
the Netherlands Nicosia

Giannoula Nathanail
executive assistant
Cyprus Clothing Industry
Association

Czech Republic
Miriam Vijfvinkel
economic and trade affairs
Embassy of the Kingdom of
the Netherlands Prague

Denmark
Søren Lester
senior policy
Embassy of the Kingdom of
the Netherlands Copenhagen

Lars K. Christensen
curator
National Museum Copenhagen

Estonia
Daan Eijwoudt
Embassy of the Kingdom of
the Netherlands Tallinn

Finland
Sini Kolehmainen
policy officer for trade & innovation
Embassy of the Kingdom of
the Netherlands Helsinki

France
Han Grooten-Feld
cultural affairs & education
Embassy of the Kingdom of
the Netherlands Paris

Nynke de Vries
press & information section
Embassy of the Kingdom of
the Netherlands Paris

Julien Payen
Centre Européen des Textiles
Innovants (CETI)

Hubert du Potet,
Union des Industries Textiles

Germany
Stefanie Streichan
culture and communication
Embassy of the Kingdom of
the Netherlands Berlin

Yolanda van Groenewoud-Jebbink,
Embassy of the Kingdom of
the Netherlands Berlin

Daniel Sonneveldt
economic department
Embassy of the Kingdom of
the Netherlands Berlin

Greece
David Röling
Embassy of the Kingdom of
the Netherlands Athens

Hungary
Éva Szabó
Embassy of the Kingdom of
the Netherlands Budapest

Szilvia Kiss-Bauer
managing director
Pannon Textile & Clothing
Cluster

Ireland
Miriam Yakop
economic and trade section
Embassy of the Kingdom of
the Netherlands Dublin

Susan Brindley
head of public affairs &
communications
Crafts Council of Ireland

Italy
Francesca Zagarese
economy, trade and agriculture
Embassy of the Kingdom of
the Netherlands Rome

Latvia
Juris Dreimanis
senior officer for trade
and promotion
Embassy of the Kingdom of
the Netherlands Riga

Darius Aukštikalnis
Lithuanian apparel and textile
industry association

Lithuania
Edvinas Varkala
senior economic and trade officer
Embassy of the Kingdom of
the Netherlands Vilnius

Luxembourg
Ank van der Biezen
Embassy of the Kingdom of
the Netherlands Luxembourg

Malta
Geert Kamminga
assistant research officer
Embassy of the Kingdom of
the Netherlands Ta' Xbiex

Professor Henry Frendo
Professor John Chircop
University of Malta

Netherlands
Babette Pörtzgen
Textiel lab Tilburg

Poland
Magdalena Cieślińska
secretariat political department
Embassy of the Kingdom of
the Netherlands Warsaw

Martin van Dijk
cultural attaché
Embassy of the Kingdom of
the Netherlands Warsaw

Daria Idsardi
trade advisor section
Embassy of the Kingdom of
the Netherlands Warsaw

Federation of Apparel & Textiles
Industry Employers (PIOT)

Portugal
Ria Bargeman
attaché for economic affairs
Embassy of the Kingdom of
the Netherlands Lisbon

Romania
Ana Androne
assistant agriculture, culture
and education
Embassy of the Kingdom of
the Netherlands Bucharest

Luiza Chiva
trade advisor
Embassy of the Kingdom of
the Netherlands Bucharest

Dorina Horatau
University of Art in Bucharest
Cristian Chesut
Universitatea de Arta si Design
Cluj-Napoca

Slovakia
Ivan Vereš
economic and trade officer
Embassy of the Kingdom of
the Netherlands Ljubljana

Slovenia
Mojca Pinterič
economic policy advisor
Embassy of the Kingdom of
the Netherlands Ljubljana

Jože Smole
officer
Branch Organisation Textile
Industry of Slovenia

Verica Zlabravec
Slovene Textile
Technology Platform

Lidija Cerne
ITGTO – University of
Ljubljana

Blaz Rat
ITGTO – University
of Ljubljana
Alenka Majcen Le Marechal
head of chair
University of Maribor

Spain
Mariska Schaap
Embassy of the Kingdom of
the Netherlands Madrid

Sweden
Eva Blom
department of economics & trade
Embassy of the Kingdom of
the Netherlands Stockholm

Frank Schipper
political affairs officer
Embassy of the Kingdom of
the Netherlands Stockholm

United Kingdom
Grant Watson
curator
Iniva (Insitute of International
Visual Arts) London